THE MARKETING BOOK

by

Jason McDonald, Ph.D.

Who say to the seers, "You must not see visions";
And to the prophets,
"You must not prophesy to us what is right,
Speak to us pleasant words,
Prophesy illusions.
Isaiah 30:10

For Ava & Hannah

COPYRIGHT AND DISCLAIMER

ACKNOWLEDGMENTS

Like any good author, I owe debts to many people. Like my Mom and Dad, who first gave me a passion to learn. Or to my first boss, Joe Warin, at Kutak, Rock & Campbell of Washington, D.C., who taught me that doing business is about helping people and having fun. Or to my wife, Noelle Decambra, who puts up with me and tells me when it's better to put up and shut up. Or to my two kids, Ava and Hannah, who both know more about Snapchat or TikTok than I ever could. Or to Gloria McNabb, who tirelessly helps me at the JM Internet Group, or to my dog, Buddy, and his pal, Levi, who walk me every day (sometimes twice a day), play ball with me and keeps me from getting heart disease at my computer. And especially, to my students at Stanford Continuing Studies and the readers of my books. You inspire me, you motivate me to be a better teacher, and you teach me more than you'll ever know

~ Jason McDonald

TABLE OF CONTENTS

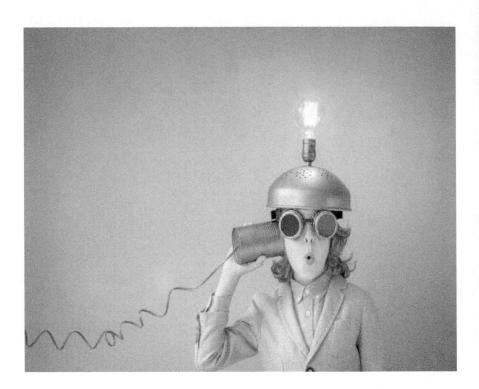

Introduction

Marketing is the art and science of "building your brand" to "sell more stuff." This book teaches the basics of marketing via the "think / do / measure" method. It will teach you **to think** like a marketer, to **make a marketing plan** for your business, and to **measure** what's working and what's not. It will help you to build your brand to sell more stuff, meaning **more sales more easily** through **better marketing**.

Let's look at the big picture.

Who Are You?

Perhaps you're a business owner or a marketing manager. Perhaps you're a salesperson or a member of a product team at a mid-sized company. Maybe you own a nail salon, a pizza restaurant, or a gym. Maybe you're an entrepreneur with an idea. Maybe you're a recent graduate with a degree in marketing who didn't learn squat in college but is now in charge of marketing for a Miami startup. Maybe you're a lawyer. *That's OK. Law firms are businesses, too (as are accounting firms and ad agencies).*

What do all these "maybes" have in common? They all want to **build their brand** and **sell more stuff**. Easily. Efficiently. Through hard work, yes, but through hard work, that's the proverbial "working smarter," not "working harder."

If you are a person who wants to "sell more stuff" by better marketing, this book is for you. If you want a quick, practical, easy-to-follow, no bullsh*t guide to marketing, this book is for you. Sorry for the profanity, but there are so many overly hyped or overly complicated guides to marketing out there, it can make one's head spin. Backwards.

Pull Off The Highway to Hell

There are too many books, too many tips, too many "new" new things - sort of like there are too many exits on the New Jersey Turnpike or Highway 101 in California.

If you've ever driven on the highway in New Jersey or California, it can be harrowing. You're speeding along. Someone (i.e., one of your competitors) is fast on your tail. You're more than a little lost. The GPS is warning you too slowly if it's working at all. Map? *Who uses a map anymore, and who can drive and look at the map at the same time?* The exits are coming up fast and whooshing by even faster. *Do you want this exit? Or that exit?* Oops, too late. It's gone.

You can crash. You can burn. Or you can just drive slowly on the highway squinting at the road signs, in "analysis paralysis" mode, as your competitors whoosh by. They exit and enter at the appropriate moments. You are overwhelmed. *There goes TikTok.* Missed it. Oops, here comes the *new Facebook interface.* Damn, missed that one, too. Here's *remarketing,* or does it say *retargeting? Branding* just zoomed by, as did our *buyer personas* and our *brand story.* Watch out! That's a *customer from hell* trying to cut us off. It's enough to make you want to give up and take the bus. Or AmTrak. But the bus sucks, and so does Amtrak. So you stay on the highway, trying to "learn marketing" while "doing marketing" in an environment of too much information too fast.

Here's what you need: a **map**, a GPS system to marketing that works. A simple **framework**. Back to the highway analogy, this book is a "rest stop," a place to pause, regroup, and learn or relearn the basics of marketing. A place to make a plan, get organized, and then get back on the "highway of marketing" to build your brand and sell more stuff.

Here's my recommendation. Pull off the "Highway to Hell" for a few hours and read this book. Your competitors, your customers, and your problems will all still be there when you finish this book. Reading this book will give you a short, simple "framework" of what marketing is and how to do it. Then, you can get back on the highway, take the right "exit," when desired, and learn more about a topic. After mastering one topic, you can get back on the highway again, and go to the next "exit," and learn what you need to do there. You will even be smart enough to skip an exit or two because they are not relevant to your business.

Who Am I?

My name is Jason McDonald. I have been doing digital marketing since 1994. I have bestselling books on Amazon on the three pillars of digital marketing: SEO, Google Ads, and Social Media Marketing. I teach digital marketing at Stanford Continuing Studies. I consult and manage several hundred thousand dollars in digital marketing efforts each month. I even do "expert witness" work when brands are naughty and step on other brands' toes online (usually trademark infringement).

I've seen the good, the bad, and the ugly. I know what works and what doesn't. I know marketing. I do marketing. I teach marketing. I love marketing!

Even better, I can explain marketing. Let's get started!

What You'll Learn

This book breaks marketing down into three key activities:

1) The Offer. First, I help you to define "what you sell" and "who wants it." This task is as much business as marketing. You will zero in on the products or services that your business offers, the customers who want what you offer, and the "unique selling proposition" that sets you above the competition.

2) Promotion. Second, I help you to brainstorm ways to promote your brand, whether customers are searching, sharing, or reviewing your products or services. The best product or service in the world means nothing if potential customers do not learn about it, get excited about it, and ultimately make a purchase!

3) Deployment. Third, I survey the most important digital opportunities that exist for today's marketers. As small business owners and marketers, we live in a very confusing time, a time of "too many" opportunities, not "too few." From SEO (Search Engine Optimization) to Social Media

Marketing, from online ads to email marketing, from traditional marketing tactics like word-of-mouth to personal selling - I give you a checklist of practical opportunities so you can identify the ones with the greatest potential to help you "build your brand" and "sell more stuff."

Twaggle: Toggling between Theory and Practice

There's also a fourth important concept, the concept of **twaggle**. Twaggle is a silly little word I created to help marketers zig and zag between "theory" and "practice," between "learning" and "doing." Twaggle is based on "toggle" (to move between activities) and action (to take action, to do something). Twaggle means that you have to have the "concept" in your head (such as knowing your brand identity) while simultaneously going out into the "real world" (such as talking with a customer face-to-face and explaining your brand to him). Twaggle means theory and practice, practice and theory, concept and action, thinking and doing, doing and thinking, measuring and learning... all at the same time. So throughout the book, I will encourage you to "twaggle," to take what you've learned and go do it, and then measure what you're doing that's working (and what's not) and revise your ideas.

Think / Do / Measure

Finally, this book teaches the **think / do / measure** method of marketing. Each Chapter teaches a marketing task by, first, explaining how to **think** about the concept, second, giving you specific to-dos to actually go **do** it, and third, providing tips on how to **measure** what's working (and what's not) to do it better over time.

Throughout the book, we'll use the example of *Jason's Cat Boarding Emporium* (JCBE), a fictitious business in San Francisco, California, that boards cats for people who are leaving the city on vacation and also offers cat grooming services as well as cat toys and paraphernalia for purchase online. As the pretend marketing manager of JCBE, we'll brainstorm ways to better market our products and services to affluent, busy San Franciscans who want to get out of town and have a place to stash the cat.

The framework of think / do / measure helps you twaggle your way to better questions, better answers, and better marketing.

Register Your Book

Register your book to get access to a PDF with easy, clickable links to all resources. In addition, you'll gain access to my companion *Marketing Almanac*, an amazing compendium of **free** marketing tools with a focus on SEO, Google Ads, and Social Media Marketing.

To register your book, go to JMLINKS.com at **http://jmlinks.com/** and entering the following JUMP CODE:

twaggle123

Next, on the landing page, re-enter "twaggle123" as the password. By registering, you'll get a PDF of the book, a template for your marketing plan, plus free access to supplementary resources in my *Marketing Almanac*.

Throughout the book, I reference external web resources using the website JMLINKS.com. Visit **http://jmlinks.com/**, enter any referenced code in the book, and you will magically be transported to the referenced website or resource.

Questions?

Got questions? Simply send me a message via **http://jmlinks.com/contact**, call 800-298-4065, or just Google "Jason McDonald" to visit my website at **https://www.jasonmcdonald.org**. Ask anything. I love questions, so don't be shy!

SECTION I
THE OFFER

In our first Section, we address a key question of marketing: defining what you sell that they want. A *good* business sells products, services, or both products and services that people actually want. A *great* business sells something that specific customers want, so passionately that they'll pay top dollar and shout the praises to the rooftops. In the Chapters that follow, I'll ask you to look deep into your marketing soul and really define your products or services, the customers who want what you sell, and what's so unique about your business that it will ignite a frenzy of demand and social sharing among your customers.

Let's get started!

Chapter 1
Write a Business Value Proposition

Writing a *Business Value Proposition* (BVP), *Elevator Pitch*, or a *Unique Selling Proposition* (USP), as this concept is sometimes called, is essential to successful marketing. The brass tacks of it is to figure out:

"What you have, that they want."

If you make **pizza**, you sell **food** to hungry **folks**. If you run a **Cat Boarding Emporium**, you sell a service to "stash the cat" to people who own a cat and want to leave town. If you make Teslas, you sell good-looking cars that convey stylish environmentalism. It's simple, and it's complicated.

In this Chapter, you will use the **think**, **do**, **measure** methodology to understand what a BVP is, to write one, and then to measure whether the BVP that's "in your head" is one that fits the "reality" of what your customers really want.

THINK: What is a BVP?

First, you need to understand what a BVP is and why a BVP is useful for your marketing. A BVP defines *what you sell that they want*. A BVP is something like "Pepsi sells soft drinks to thirsty young consumers, as the choice of a new generation," or "Tesla sells electric cars to affluent consumers who are both eco-friendly and desirous of sporty, good-looking vehicles." For our hypothetical *Jason's Cat Boarding Emporium*, we might write a simple BVP as follows:

Jason's Cat Boarding Emporium sells cat boarding to folks in San Francisco who are leaving town and need a place to stash their cats. We also sell cat toys and paraphernalia online, plus offer cat grooming services to luxury-minded cat lovers in the City by the Bay.

We will drill down to a more detailed Business Value Proposition in a moment, but for now, just notice that the BVP explains "what we sell" "that they want." You don't need to overcomplicate it. The best BVPs are short, sweet, and – more important - **specific**. If you find yourself writing empty marketing platitudes like "amazing customer service" or "high-value services," take those out. Make every word matter.

Notice also that a BVP implicitly or explicitly references "buyer personas," that is, it explains specifically *who* wants what you have. (We'll discuss *buyer personas* in more detail in the next Chapter). If you find yourself writing a BVP yet wondering who wants it or realizing that the customer might "want it" but not yet "know it," don't freak out. Just realize that being innovative has its pluses and its minuses. Henry Ford once said, "If I had asked people what they wanted, they would have said faster horses;" people wanted transportation; they just didn't (yet) realize that they wanted cars.

Another term that you may hear is *USP* or *Unique Selling Proposition*. Whereas a BVP emphasizes what you sell and who wants it, a USP assumes that you already know this and instead focuses on what's unique about what you're selling. USPs build on the marketing concept of **positioning**. Positioning answers the question, "What's unique about your product or service vs. that of the competition?" (We'll cover positioning in more detail in **Chapter 4**).

For now, let's return to how the USP builds off of, yet is different from the BVP. For example, the BVP of both Pepsi and Coke is a carbonated sugar-filled beverage that quenches thirst, yet the USP of the one is different from the other. Pepsi is often positioned as the soda for a "new generation," whereas Coca-Cola is positioned as a "classic" American drink. They're both soft drinks, but the former attempts to speak to the future, that is, young people who want something new and different, whereas the latter attempts to speak, not so much to the past, but to the idea of classic American values, something quintessentially American. Pepsi is also sweeter than Coke, so the product itself also reflects a unique selling position.

What's an "elevator pitch?" You may hear this term as well. An "elevator pitch" is really just a combined BVP and USP stated in a very short fashion, the idea being you can "pitch" it to someone as you ride an elevator from the 21st floor to the lobby. So the "elevator pitch" for Pepsi might be, "We're a carbonated cola, slightly sweeter than Coca-Cola, that's the taste of a new generation." The "elevator pitch" for Jason's Cat Boarding Emporium might be, "We board cats for busy San Franciscans who want a place to stash the cat, plus we sell luxury cat toys and paraphernalia online, and offer premium cat grooming to San Francisco cat lovers."

I think it's easier to write one BVP that contains in it the idea of your positioning – what's unique about your product or service, rather than to write a BVP and a USP. So I just write BVPs. I also highly recommend that they be short, sweet, and to the point. Think "elevator pitch," not "Ph.D. dissertation." Don't get hung up on nomenclature.

A BVP needs to answer three questions:

1) What do you sell?

2) Who wants it?

3) What's unique about what you offer vs. the competition?

DO: Write Your BVP

In the Chapters that follow, we will drill into the concepts of a BVP in even more detail. But in this Chapter, let's get at your to-dos at a high level of generality. First, what do you sell? Is it a product or a service? Or perhaps both? For Jason's Cat Boarding Emporium, for example, we sell physical **products** like cat toys, cat food, or perhaps cat carriers. These are tangible products. But we also sell **services**, like cat boarding, cat grooming, or seminars on how to care for your cats, or even workshops for employers on the value of having pets in the workplace. For your own BVP, your first to-do is to formulate a very specific statement of the products and/or services that you sell.

Next, you want to drill down into who wants what you have. This has to do with your **customer segments** or **buyer personas**. "Customer segments" is just marketing speak for the groups of people who want what you have. One aspect of customer segments is *demographics*. Demographics are relatively stable attributes such as *male* versus *female*, or *old* people vs. *young* people, etc. *Psychographics*, as the name implies, have to do with psychology. These are people who love cats versus people who love dogs. Technically speaking, a cat lover can become a dog lover, whereas a man cannot generally become a woman, or an old person become a young person. So demographics refer to fixed attributes of your target customers, whereas psychographics refers to psychological attributes that are "in the mind."

Next, there are *situational* aspects. An example would be people who are leaving town and need a place to stash their cats. This is a situation that propels people to look for cat boarding. Finally, there are *economic* attributes, such as rich people for whom price is no object versus poor people who are price-sensitive. As you write your BVP, you want to keep an eye on your customer segments. Your to-do here is to implicitly or explicitly include a statement of your target customers in your finished BVP.

In **Chapter 2,** we will discuss *buyer personas*, which are more detailed sketches of your potential customers.

Finally, focus on the question of "what's unique about what you have?" There is more than one cat boarding establishment in San Francisco, so we have to explain why they should choose us and not the competition. Our answer is that we're focused on *luxury*. We're not cheap. We're luxurious and provide your cat with only the best in cat grooming and cat boarding services for cats (and people) for whom money is no object. This contrasts with cheap cat boarding services, which focus on the low end of the market. It's not that one is good and one bad; rather, you have to focus and be unique. So your third to-do is to get uniqueness into your BVP. What's unique about what you sell? Be specific.

Your final business value proposition should be about two to three sentences long and should be specific without being redundant. Here's a revised business value proposition for Jason's Cat Boarding Emporium.

"Jason's Cat Boarding Emporium of San Francisco offers premium cat boarding services to affluent and busy San Franciscans who need a place for their cats. In addition to boarding, we offer grooming and cat-training services. We also sell cat-related products like collars, cat toys, and cat food, both in San Francisco and online. Finally, we offer cat training sessions and even workshops for Bay Area businesses who want to train their employees on the value of pets in the workplace."

Notice how it explains what we sell, the different customer segments who want our products and services, and what's unique about us.

MEASURE: Revise Your BVP

Your BVP is not "set in stone." It's not something that you write and set aside. Rather, the twaggle is to keep your BVP in mind yet go out into the world to figure out if what you think you are selling is resonating with real customers. Twaggle between your concept of what you sell and the reality of what they want. Don't abandon your vision, but don't ignore reality either. Don't be afraid to be like Henry Ford or Steve Jobs. A brilliant entrepreneur knows what customers need or want before they do, and he persuades them into his vision. That's what Elon Musk of Tesla is trying to do in today's electric car market. (We'll see if he succeeds – stay tuned).

So, after you've written your BVP and you start marketing, it's time to **measure**. Because the BVP is a relatively general concept, you want to keep it in the back of your mind at all times. Does it accurately describe what you sell? Does it capture your target customer segments? Does it convey what's unique about your products and/or services? These are not static, eternal questions. These are ongoing questions about your business and marketing, and the answers can, and should, be constantly evaluated and revised. Like a good scientist, compare your BVP against reality and revise accordingly.

You might abandon products or services that no one wants, for example. Or you might revise your BVP as you discover new products or services that make you a lot of money. Perhaps the money really isn't in cat *grooming*; it's in cat *boarding*. Perhaps the money is now in *marijuana cat treats*, as San Francisco embraces legal marijuana. Times change, and so will your product, service, and marketing mix. Look for opportunities!

Also, keep an eye on buyer personas, that is, which customer types really respond to what you're selling, and which ones do not. Look for patterns. When any customer comes into your store or buys what you have online, try to evaluate him or her as an archetype of a specific customer segment. Is he a man or a woman? Rich or poor? Someone who is situationally compelled to find cat boarding at the last minute, or someone who wants a long-term relationship for cat grooming? What's "in his mind" that has driven him to reach out to your business?

Looking ahead, you might realize that you have the best product or service in the world, you have defined customer segments who really want it, and you have a unique selling proposition. Everything is working, yet you're not selling enough stuff. What's going wrong? Here, you can run up against something that is pure marketing: the marketing message. It might be that your marketing message or promotional efforts are the problem. The twaggle is to see how everything fits together and be able to debug what's going wrong, whether it's product or service, customer segments, unique selling proposition, or the message itself.

Marketing (like business in general) is never "finished." Brainstorm, deploy, measure - then rinse and repeat!

Chapter 2
Identify Your Buyer Personas

One of the newer words to enter the marketing lexicon is "buyer personas" or "customer personas." In the old days, like three or four years ago, marketers used to talk about "customer segments." The word you use isn't as important as the concept, namely to look at your company, product, or service from the "outside in," from the perspective of potential customers. **Who are your customers?** What do they want? And how do they clump into definable groups? How can organizing your customers into definable personas help you to better tune your marketing to their hopes, needs, dreams, and fears?

THINK: Who Are Your Customers Segments and Buyer Personas?

Let's take a step back from buyer personas and talk first about **customer segments**. "Customer segments" is the broad-brush term by which marketers conceptualize who wants or buys the stuff they're ultimately selling. One fundamental way to think about customer segments is to group your customers by attributes or dimensions that are "permanent" or "very hard to change" vs. attributes or dimensions that are "not-so-permanent" or "easy to change."

For example, *demographics* goes into the first type. Men don't generally become women, rich people don't generally become poor, and persons who live in Texas don't generally become persons who live in California. These hard-to-change dimensions then give you some predictive power on customer wants, pain points, or behaviors. If your company is selling prenatal photography, for example, the primary customer will be women (since men don't generally have babies), and if you are selling University of Oklahoma sports paraphernalia, you can be pretty sure that folks in Texas won't want it, and won't buy it. Income level is another relatively stable attribute. Rich people, generally speaking, are much more likely to buy luxury cars than poor people, and poor people spend a higher proportion of their income on Ubers, Lyfts, and bus tickets.

If *demographics* speaks to hard-to-change attributes of your customer segmentation, then *psychographics* speaks to easier-to-change attributes. People who "lean left" tend to like organic food more than people who "lean right," for example. (Why I'm not sure, but it does seem to be true). But that attribute is more "in their head" than something in the physical reality around them, like what sex they are or whether they are rich or poor. People can be persuaded to try organic food even if they "lean right" or "are poor," and diet fads from weight loss programs, to avocado-is-good-for-you, to gluten-is-bad-for-you speak more to the psychology of customers than to their demographics (though not entirely). Psychographics, in short, describe psychological elements and lifestyles – aspects that are more fluid than demographics.

Another element to figuring out your customer personas is *situational*. People who are in their 20's, for example, tend to be out on the dating scene, consuming movies and restaurant meals more than people in their 50s. The "situation" is as critical as the "age." Think "people who are single" vs.

"people who are married." Or a situational is "people who are in Palo Alto and are hungry," or "people in the market for a new car" or "people who have just bought movie tickets," and you can predict that they might be good targets for popcorn. People who are leaving town and need a place to stash the cat are "situationally" primed to purchase from Jason's Cat Boarding Emporium.

You can pretty easily see that the line between demographics, or "hard-to-change," and psychographics or "easy-to-change," is blurrier than you might think at first glance. But psychographic or situational attributes such as Republican vs. Democrat, open-to-change vs. tradition-minded, just-had-a-baby vs. in-retirement are important elements to consider as you map out your customer groups.

Finally, consider the position of your customers on the **customer journey** as well, which is really a situational aspect. You have *prospects* (people who are out there who "qualify" as someone who might be interested in your product or service) vs. *customers* (people who have actually made a purchase) to *superfans* (people who have purchased from you and love you so much they'll post a review on Yelp, create a YouTube video, or tell their friends and family via word-of-mouth as to how fantastic you are). You also have disgruntled customers who are so unhappy that they will post a negative review or tell everyone they know that your product or service sucks. I call these people "customers from hell," and they are (unfortunately) very powerful in today's age of Internet reviews. In short, you want to encourage *prospects* to become *customers* and *customers* to become *superfans* while mitigating any "customers from hell" (by fixing their problems, preferably before they start).

As a marketer, you want to research and understand how the *situation* a customer finds him or herself in can chart their desires and pain points. People who bring their cats into Jason's Cat Emporium on a regular basis, i.e., our "existing customers," are a very different lot than those who find us on Google from a search for "cat boarding in San Francisco." The former know us (and hopefully love us), whereas the latter are skeptical and need to be persuaded to make that first purchase of San Francisco's premium cat boarding experience.

With these concepts in your head, return to the new notion of **buyer personas**. Think of a customer or buyer persona as if you were role-playing or dressing up for theater as an actor. It's the total package; demographics, psychographics, and even situational. So, to take Jason's Cat Boarding Emporium as an example, we might conceptualize a "customer persona" of the busy downtown worker, affluent and in their twenties, who has one cat. He frequently travels because he's at the stage of life of heavy dating and friend orientation, and he wants a convenient, high-quality cat boarding service. Free cat pickup at his apartment would be a plus because he's affluent and pressed for time.

This contrasts with a San Francisco mom who has a husband, two kids, and a dog *and* a cat. She travels less frequently but for longer periods of time and is more likely to be price-sensitive as she has an entire family to deal with, including a dog. A service that dealt with both cats and dogs might be quite appealing, or a pet sitting service that comes into the home might be even better. Woman, man, rich, poor, frequent traveler vs. infrequent traveler, living alone and thus a sole decision-maker, vs. living in a family and thus facing group dynamics - these jumbles of attributes, taken together, make up a *buyer persona*.

You can literally visualize in your head the twenty-something office worker vs. the harried mom, and that's the point of buyer personas - to help you see the world (and your product or service) from their perspective. "Outside looking in" is the operative concept. How might they look for what you offer? How sensitive are they to online reviews or the word-of-mouth of friends and family? What are their desires or pain points, and how do these correlate with your product or service features and benefits? Buyer personas are a shorthand way of bundling together the elements of demographics, psychographics, and situationality, to help you be better at marketing to what each "group" has in common. It's a way to see patterns among your customers and then tune your marketing to the hopes, fears, needs, and wants of each pattern.

DO: Sketch out Your Own Buyer Personas

You probably already have a gut instinct of who your customers are and even how they clump together into definable personas. Your **to-do** here is to formalize this. First and foremost, do some market research. If you're already in business, consider polling your existing customers and asking them about demographic, psychographic, and situational aspects. A survey might ask, "What brought you to the Cat Emporium today?" "Can you tell us your income level, sex, and family status?," and then ask questions such as "Which is more important to you, low cost or a higher quality cat experience such as a private cage, or as we like to call it a 'hotel room?'" or "Would you like to include grooming at the end of your cat stay?"

By asking questions like these, you can slice and dice your customers and see patterns - perhaps people who work downtown tend to be interested in pickup and delivery of their cats, vs. people who live in the more suburban parts of San Francisco are more interested in a home visitation service. This will tell you where to offer which service and where to advertise or promote each service. Perhaps men are more interested in price, and women in quality (or vice-versa). Buyer personas do tend to be a bit like stereotyping, so just remember that - ultimately — each of us is an individual, even if we share predictable affinities. How many folks who love to eat organic kale voted for the Republican candidate? Or how many gun owners prefer Whole Foods to Walmart? Some things do seem to go together, even if it's a mystery why. You get the picture; you can predict one thing from knowing another, even though it's a probability and not a certainty.

If you're not already in business, you may need to use the Internet to research what's potentially out there. Use tools like the *Answer the Public* (**https://answerthepublic.com/**) to research keywords, and then ask yourself what each search query tells you about a potential customer group. Look for Facebook groups, groups on LinkedIn, or even trending hashtags on Twitter and Instagram for clues as to how your customers clump into definable buyer personas. "Birds of a feather flock together," as they say. Finally, gather your team, brainstorm, and sketch out your potential buyer personas. Hubspot offers some excellent free "persona templates" at **http://jmlinks.com/41u**. Download those and go to work.

At the end of this exercise, you should end up with from one to ten "buyer personas." You and your marketing team should be able to mentally put "on" the mask of one of your personas and see the world from their perspective. What are their desires vis-a-vis your product or service? What are their pain points? What aspects of your product or service really turn them on, and which aspects give them anxiety? Why? Do they make decisions as an individual, or perhaps are they an influencer or someone who is influenced by influencers? Do they search for your product, or are they more likely to discover it after a recommendation from a friend, family, or colleague?

Some companies even give names to their buyer personas, such as "John, the busy office worker," and "Sally, the harried San Francisco mom." You might even discover "negative" personas, types of persons who might find out about or use your product but are unlikely to buy it, or if they do, unlikely to be happy with it. These are the folks who will "go negative" against you on the Internet, writing negative reviews on Yelp or trashing you on YouTube. Even a negative customer persona can be helpful as you plan out your marketing strategy to attract likely, happy buyers and repel unlikely, unhappy customers.

MEASURE: Be Sensitive to Changing Buyer Personas

Researching and creating customer personas is a key part of marketing research. So think of this in phases. In Phase I, you search, brainstorm, and do your best to create a map of your buyer personas. Then, in Phase II, as you serve real customers and do real marketing, you measure your personas against reality. Have you captured the key types? Do you know their key desires, pain points, and attributes (demographic, psychographic, and situational)? What did you "get right," and what did you "get wrong?" Revise your personas accordingly.

By measuring your pre-conceived notion of buyer personas against reality, you might discover new attributes or even entirely new customer personas. It's helpful to have a formal Word or Google doc where you give names to your personas, and you meet regularly with your team - perhaps once a month or once a quarter - to evaluate whether you have a good handle on the most important buyer personas, whether you need to refine them, or whether you've even discovered new ones. Be attuned to changes in demographics, psychographics, and situations as customer personas and the "real" people or groups they represent can evolve over time. Years ago, no one liked kale, and now it seems to define a whole subculture. Go figure.

Chapter 3
Build Your Brand

T he word *brand* comes from an Old English word for "burning." Even today, we describe the rather barbaric process by which cattle become "marked" by hot iron as "branding," and the "logo," as it were, that appears on each cow, as a "brand." A brand originally marked ownership, but over time, branding has come to mean the "warm and fuzzy" feeling a consumer associates with a particular company and its products or services. Cattle from Rancher "A," for example, are supposed to be better tasting than cattle from Rancher "B," just like a Cabernet wine from Vineyard "A" is supposed to taste better than a Cabernet from Vineyard "B." The brand conveys something you can count on, a prediction you can make about a product or service before you try it or buy it. It's the warm and fuzzy that extends before, during, and after a purchase.

To be more current than cows and cabernets, take a look at Apple. Notice, for example, that the first thing that popped into your head wasn't the shiny red fruit but the Cupertino-based technology company, i.e., Apple computer. Apple has a brand *identity*. Apple has brand *equity*. And Apple has worked hard at *branding*, the process of projecting brand identity, and building brand equity into the minds of its target customers.

THINK: Brands are Built One Marketing Decision at a Time

Brands are the personalities of businesses. They are the warm and fuzzy feeling you have around a company that pre-positions you as ready to buy their products or services. A brand identity like Rolex means stylish, quality watches that say "you've made it," and you can afford the incredible price. A brand like Walmart, in contrast, means you're a smart shopper who knows value when she sees it. And a brand like Tesla means cars that are not only eco-friendly but prestigiously sporty. **Brand identity**, in the abstract, is that "warm and fuzzy" feeling you have around a company. It pre-sells you. It primes you to think positively, and it makes the sales process easier for the company. That's why companies strive to create and nurture positive brands; they make it easier to sell more stuff and make more money.

Notice as well that the brand rubs off on the consumer. Those who drive Teslas are environmentally conscious, wealthy, and stylish. The **brand halo** envelopes the consumer. Tribal animals that we humans are, we want to get "inside of" brands that conform with our own personal identities. Consumers "fall for" the idea that you are what you drive, you are what brand of cell phone or computer you use, or you are whom you vote for. Tribalism is the psychological footprint of the dance between consumer and brand.

If a brand is the *static* result of all the hard work of the marketing department, **branding** is the art of building a brand one marketing step at a time. Let's look at branding step by step. First, you have to define your **brand identity**. This is the complex of *skills* and *attributes* that you want to associate with your company. Skills are not the same as attributes; the former refers to the technical things your company can do, and the latter refers to the idiosyncratic aspects of personality. Tesla, for example, has the "skill" of making eco-friendly, fun, and stylish cars. The cars will get you where you want to go and do it without polluting (*the skills*) but also wrap a halo around you as an eco-friendly, smart, and stylish consumer (*the attributes*). The Tesla brand is a "helpful expert" to assist you in building your own personal brand, and the Tesla branding project is the struggle to persuade you as a consumer that this is the best car for the job.

Return to your own company and your own Business Value Proposition. Examine it now from the perspective of branding. What *skills* does your company, product, or service provide? These are the technical aspects. What *attributes* characterize your company? These are your brand personality. At Jason's Cat Boarding Emporium, for example, our "skills" are that we know how to board cats properly and safely. Our "attributes" are our personality as the luxury, spare-no-expense part of our brand that means money is no object (for you, your cat, and us). Brand identity, in other words, always combines skills and attributes, with skills being practical things that the company can "do" for its customers and the attributes being more the personality traits that it and its customers share as values. Apple users believe not only that Apple products are useful, stylish, and well-designed; they believe that they, too, are stylish and well-designed consumers.

Stop here for a second, and notice the dance between "reality" and the "brand." If Apple products weren't actually easy-to-use, then the consumer backlash would eat away and perhaps destroy the brand. If a company becomes embroiled in corruption, as both Volkswagen and Wells Fargo have been recently, then the brand image of honesty can be destroyed. How can you trust a German car maker that cheated on emission tests? How can you trust a bank that incentivized employees to sell customers products that they did not need? The road to *trust* is a long and hard one; the road to *mistrust* is quick and down abruptly. **Brand equity** is the built-up trust in a company. It can be very positive (Apple) or pretty negative (the IRS). Like a bank account, brands can draw it down due to scandal or poor products. Like a bank account, brands can build it up by being socially positive or creating great products.

Next comes **brand iconography**. Iconography is the graphics, text, and narrative that surround the brand and communicate its personality. (Religious experience comes to mind; the iconography of the Catholic Church is different from that of the Baptists, and the iconography of the Baptists is different from that of the Muslims or Atheists). In business, look at Apple's logo, for example. It is simple, clean, and stylish. Apple products themselves "look" simple, clean, and stylish. Every effort is made to make them easy-to-use, and every marketing icon from the clean, uncluttered look of the Apple Store to the clean, uncluttered look of the Apple iPhone works to unify graphics, narrative, and text. The iconography of the Apple brand builds out the brand in the physical world and in the digital / mental world of communication and advertising.

Brand consistency is part of branding. It is the conscious effort to make every communicative or iconic aspect of the company work towards the desired brand identity. It's no accident that Steve Jobs and current CEO Tim Cook dress in sleek black clothes, have stylish but subdued haircuts, and wear expensive designer eyeglasses. Even their look on stage is part of Apple's brand projection and Apple's branding, the company's systematic effort to project a consistent brand identity.

Not all companies succeed at coherent branding. Compare Apple's brand *consistency*, for example, to Google's brand *inconsistency*. First, Google called its local product "Google local," then "Google+ Local," and now "Google My Business." First, it was AdWords, and now it's Google Ads. Every day there's a new "Google Doodle," which you could argue confuses the Google logo and brand image (even if it attempts to build a larger brand of social activism). First, it was Google, and now it's Alphabet. Compare how every Chik-fil-A or In-N-Out Burger has the same clean look, and yet how one Burger King or KFC is pretty nice, and another is a disastrous mess. **Brand consistency** supports **brand identity** (or it doesn't).

Finally, **promotion** is a key part of branding. A conceptualized brand identity and defined brand iconography are all for naught if they are not projected into the culture. One of the biggest jobs of the marketing department – if not *the* biggest job – is to build the brand by promoting the brand systematically and by all available means. The tools here are things like the look, feel, and function of the website, the photos used in social media marketing, participation at industry trade shows, white papers, webinars, and other events, etc. This includes as well all efforts at public relations, such as media interviews, white papers, and other "free" attempts at so-called "earned media." And this means as well all advertising efforts whether those ads appear in print, on billboards, on television, on Google or Bing, on YouTube or Snapchat. It even means the design of products and packaging, the employee uniforms, or even how the employees talk with customers.

Visit your neighborhood Chik-fil-A restaurant, for example, and observe how the employees do not say, "You're welcome," but rather "My pleasure." This is by design and by training, and it promotes the Chik-fil-A brand as a cut above McDonald's and Burger King, whose employees often do not even seem to know the phrase, "You're welcome." The cleanliness of Chik-fil-A is also another brand signifier. Have you ever compared the restrooms at Chik-fil-A to those at Burger King? If you have, as I have, I feel sorry for you. If you haven't and you're brave, try using the restroom at Burger King and then at Chik fil A. Even the restrooms convey a brand identity, such as cleanliness down to attention to detail.

Branding is for Everyone. Should you think that branding is only for big companies, think again. Any successful company down to the smallest artisan coffee shop or bread baker in your neighborhood, or the local dentist or real estate agent, or even the manufacturer of superglues or other adhesives – any successful company has a brand identity and engages in branding. Even small companies project a brand identity!

Now, whether it is coherent or not, whether it is effective or not, whether it is done well or not – these are separate questions. The real world is messy. Some companies are skillful, and some companies are clueless. Brand identities can be vague or unstable, the efforts at branding can be ineffective or incoherent, and promotion efforts can be haphazard. As Voltaire quipped, "The perfect is the enemy of the good." The essential takeaway about branding is that you project a brand image *whether you want to or not*. Just as there is no person without a personality, there is no company without a brand. Some are strong, crisp, and valuable. Some are weak, fuzzy, and detrimental. But all companies project a brand identity without exception.

Brand equity, in summary, is the positive brand identity that one has in the virtual "bank" of customers' minds. It's the idea that when Apple releases a new product, it will probably be very good; it's the positive "benefit of the doubt" that Apple enjoys. Brand equity speaks to how a positive brand makes all of sales and marketing easier. Negative brand equity like a brand such as Wells Fargo, Volkswagen, Burger King, or KFC means that the brand is "in the hole" and has to work its way back up to a positive reputation among consumers. Positive brand equity helps you sell more stuff, and negative brand equity makes it more difficult. Regardless, your job as a marketer is to build up your brand so as to make sales easier.

DO: Build, Promote, and Protect Your Brand

"Begin with the end in mind" is habit #2 of Stephen Covey's *7 Habits of Highly Effective People*. So your first **to-do** is to define your **brand identity**. This can be incorporated into your Business Value Proposition; just remember the difference between "skills" and "attributes." Skills speak to the "left brain" logical things you can do for a target customer; attributes speak to the "right brain" personality aspects of whether your brand is cool or practical, luxurious or cheap, eco-friendly, or a muscle car. Return to your buyer personas, your positioning statement, and define a brand identity with your team that combines skills and attributes. For Jason's Cat Boarding Emporium, for example, we would define our *skills* as efficient and safe cat boarding and our *attributes* as luxury, spare-no-expense, high-end quality for the discriminating cat owner. We are the *Nieman Marcus* of cat boarding in San Francisco, not the *Kmart*.

Next, brainstorm your **brand iconography**, starting with your company logo. As an icon of your brand, your logo should convey who you are, what you do, and how you are unique in a positive way. Beyond your logo, every other piece of marketing collateral, from the color schemes used on your website to perhaps even how your employees answer the phone, should communicate your brand identity. Iconography should be defined, and a consistent look and feel should operate throughout your products or services. Iconography isn't just the visuals, however. It is also the way you write or talk; a *cowboy* brand speaks differently than a New York City *elitist* brand.

Finally, with *brand identity* and *brand iconography* defined, turn to **brand promotion**. The to-dos here are complex. In fact, promoting your brand image in a systematic way is perhaps the most time-consuming to-do in all of marketing. Every piece of content that is produced as part of your content marketing should work towards a consistent brand image. Every advertisement you run, every webinar you give, every menu you produce if you are a restaurant, or every email you send if you are an accountant should project and promote your brand identity. Every employee should be trained in the company culture and how to project a positive brand image in every face-to-face interaction. Brand identity runs like a literary theme through all of marketing communications, and the most powerful and successful brands deploy their brand identity in a way so systematic that customers immediately "know" when they are experiencing the brand from the first minute of the first encounter. The twaggle of brand promotion is to project a consistent brand identity into the culture day in and day out.

MEASURE: Does your Brand Support Your Sales?

Marketing is the art and science of creating an environment around your business (a.k.a., your "brand") that makes it easier to sell more stuff. The ultimate metric to judge your brand is whether it is helping (or hurting) your sales efforts and by how much. Don't fall into the trap of thinking branding is only for "big companies." Don't think you can't measure your brand. It's either helping make sales easier, or it's hurting.

Accordingly, the "measure" element of brand-building is a drill-down to: a) **brand awareness** – are your target customers aware of your brand at all?, b) **brand attributes** – do your target customers perceive your brand in a positive light?, c) **brand equity** – does your brand for the company as a whole assist with new product and/or service launches, and d) **brand effectiveness**, does your brand ultimately make sales easier? Don't miss so-called *reputation management*, which generally refers to monitoring one's online brand image and attempting to prevent or repair any attacks against it. If branding is *offense*, reputation management is *defense*.

How will you monitor your brand reputation and prevent (or defend) negative brand events?

You can deconstruct and measure branding into each of these aspects, as well as return to the beginning and ask whether the brand identity you originally conceived is the most effective one for projecting positivity and selling more stuff. Your brand exists not only in your own mind but in the minds of your customers, and the measurement questions are whether the desired brand image gets projected at all, whether it's positive or negative, and whether your brand helps you to sell more stuff.

Chapter 4
Position Your Product or Service

Your product or service doesn't live in a vacuum. It will compete against other products or services in a crowded marketplace. The customer will wonder, "What's unique about it?" and "Why should I choose you over a competitor?" *Positioning* is the struggle to define what's unique and compelling against competitive choices. "Choose me!" your marketing message will shout. "Why?" the customer will ask. "Here's why," you will answer.

Positioning is a key part of your answer.

THINK: Positioning is Part Reality and Part Perception

Cars are an easy example of how positioning blends reality and perception. *Porsche*, for example, is positioned at the high-end of the car market, not so much as a luxury vehicle as much as a sports vehicle. Compare that to *Lexus*, which is decidedly a luxury brand, or *Hyundai*, which occupies the low-end, value end of the market. Do this mental exercise: list car brands in your head (*Chevy, Ford, BMW, Lexus, Toyota, Tesla, Nissan,* etc.), and notice how you can literally chart them on a matrix from *cheap* to *expensive*, *luxury* to *sporty* to *economy*. You can quickly see that they are "positioned" in the marketplace against other brands and against customer needs or segments. Busy moms and dads need Chrysler Minivans, and affluent empty-nesters might want a sports vehicle like a Porsche 911. Are cars really different? Yes and no. Minivans do have more space. A Porsche really can drive faster than a Hyundai. But, as my Dad says, they all have four wheels and get you from point "A" to point "B." There's a mixture of reality and perception in the car market, and that's positioning at work.

Or, take groceries, and you can position *Whole Foods* vs. *Safeway* vs. *Albertsons* vs. *Sprouts* vs. *Trader Joe's* vs. *Star Market* vs. *Giant* vs. *your local organic grocery that's not a chain* or *your local farmer's market* and see that in the crowded grocery store marketplace, competing brands are positioned against each other. If "position" speaks to their relatively stable location, "positionING" speaks to how the marketing staff at a company attempts to fortify their position, and "repositioning" speaks to when a company, product, or service is not satisfied with its position and seeks to move towards a new one.

An example of repositioning would be how Whole Foods, now that it is owned by Amazon, is trying to reposition itself away from the high-end, organic part of the market and towards the lower-end, value part of the market. Will it work? Will Whole Foods be perceived as a high-end grocer or a value grocer? Can it be both? Here's a fun fact. Trader Joe's, which is positioned at the high(er) end of the organic "foodie" market, is actually owned by Aldi, which positions itself at the low end of the grocery market for value-conscious consumers. I doubt many snobs who shop at Whole Foods and Trader Joe's even know that Aldi actually owners Trader Joe's, but it does.

Brand confusion is the danger here. Trader Joe's and Aldi keep their relationship (relatively) secret for a reason. They don't want to confuse people or cross-contaminate the brands.

Whether Whole Foods can retain its positioning as an ecofriendly, high-end food store yet be owned by the "evil" (in quotes) Jeff Bezos is a similar problem. Positioning speaks to the problem that you "can't be all things to all people." You have to make choices and define yourself.

Digging into "positioning," you should ask, "positioned against what?" It's not just against the competition. It's also against categories, product benefits or features, or even situations. First, you have to do your market research and understand what matters from the perspective of your customer. Positioning answers the question "What's unique about you?" or "Where do you stand against 'x,' with 'x,' being an attribute such as price, value, sportiness, organic vs. non-organic, or whatever attributes are relevant to your target customers.

Most of us will position with respect to other competitors in the marketplace, but you can also position against other attributes. Thus we have:

positioning against the competition;

positioning against a category;

positioning against a product or service feature or benefit; and

positioning against a situation.

For example, first-class air travel is positioned against business class or coach. You might not know how much "better" first-class is if you couldn't look down the aisles at the miserable people in coach. In fact, you could even argue that the airlines need to mix first class and coach in the same airplane so that the one looks "value-conscious" and the other looks "luxury conscious." Here, the positioning of first class on United Airlines is thus against another product of the same company, its business or coach class. This is situational positioning.

Indeed, United Airlines as a whole is positioned against Southwest, which has no classes, or JetBlue, which has sleeper pods and free TV. When Southwest touts the fact that "bags fly free," it's positioning itself against competitors, not as a whole, but against the very concept of whether we should, or should not, have to pay to check bags. Spirit Airlines, in contrast, is positioned as the ultra-low-cost carrier, charging for everything up to and including printing a boarding pass or taking carry-on luggage on board. Spirit Airlines is positioned against the other airlines but also against the concept of what air travel "is," namely is it a bundle of services such as checked bags, carry-on bags, seat assignments, etc., that can never be unbundled? Or is it a set of services that you can unbundle? Its positioning is fly cheap and pay as you go. Fortunately, the CEO has indicated that "bathrooms are not a choice." At least, not yet. Spirit Airlines is an example of positioning against a category, "air travel," and arguing that it's really more than one category.

Throughout, you'll see that a lot of positioning speaks to features or benefits. You either offer this or that, or you don't. Either you're Safeway (a high-end grocer), and they'll help carry your bags to your car, or you're Food for Less (a low-end grocer), and you bag them yourself and push your cart to your car by yourself. Either you're a Lexus with seat warmers, or you're a low-end Nissan, and you roll up your window manually. Forget about seat warmers.

Notice when it comes to airlines that we see, again, the marketing theme of reality vs. the message. The reality is that Southwest does not charge for two checked bags – that's a product or service choice. But the messaging as conveyed in advertising that "bags fly free" is a choice made not in reality but in the message. As the marketing manager, you can tweak the actual product or service, or just the messaging, or both. You can even tweak the **brand messaging** through advertising, organic efforts on social media, and public relations without changing anything in "reality" at all. In the marketplace for bottled water, for example, a fierce battle rages that one company's H2O is quite different from the other company's H2O. In other words, don't get hung up on reality as you write your positioning statement!

Another aspect of positioning is positioning by price. Televisions, for example, will often be positioned as cheap ones, with few features, against expensive ones, with many features. They sit on the same shelf to "help us" (very much in quotes) figure out which television to buy. This is also called "anchoring," the market strategy that reflects Goldilocks – not too cheap, not too expensive, but just right – all created "by design" and effective marketing. Here again, notice that the reality of price isn't the same as the messaging of price; pricing is a marketing decision that is as much communication as it is reality.

Walk into your local Best Buy and browse TVs, or go online and do the same on Amazon. You'll see the high price, the low price, and the Goldilocks price. If you pay attention, you may even notice the "price illusion" that higher-priced items must be better than lower priced items. You see this all the time in the wine market. There's the really cheap wine (which must be bad), the really expensive wine (which must be good), and the middle-priced wine (which is good enough for your mother-in-law). The blur of all this pricing chatter is the struggle of positioning.

Perceptual maps are a fancy way of putting onto paper how your product or service is positioned. This is often done on a matrix. So, to take cars as an example, you can take out a piece of paper, and on the "x" axis put "cheap" to "expensive," and on the "y" access put "luxury" to "sport." You can then scatter chart the car brands and see where each "lives" against these attributes. More formally, you might survey your customers or even conduct a focus group to research how they "perceive" different brands in the marketplace and how they are positioned against each other and against whatever attributes happen to be important to your target customers. Here again, you are focused not only on reality but also on perception.

Marketing works ultimately in the mind and not in reality, and so does positioning. In fact, marketers might argue that perception IS reality, so as you work on positioning, you get to its final element: messaging. Your market message or "positioning statement" might take as much into account that has to do with perceptions and the projected brand image you want to create as to the reality. The "Febreze" cleaning product, for example, was originally positioned as a cleaner of smells (and failed) and then was repositioned as a mini-reward at the end of the cleaning cycle and succeeded (See **http://jmlinks.com/41v**). The point here is that Febreze - the product - in reality, didn't change at all. What changed was the marketing of it and the consumer perception - all a function of effective positioning and messaging by the Febreze marketing team.

DO: Write a Positioning Statement for Your Product or Service

Your to-dos are first to research the competitive landscape and second to write a "positioning statement:"

Which competitive products or services are already in the marketplace?

Which features or benefits are desired by the target customers?

Which needs or desires are being effectively served? Which ones are not being addressed?

How is each competitor positioned against the others and against key customer desires or needs?

Where are there opportunities to serve an "unaddressed" niche?

Your finished positioning statement should answer the customer question, "Why should I choose you over them?" Your completed positioning statement can and should blend both the "reality" and the "perceptual" elements of your product or service.

MEASURE: Be Ready to Reposition

Things change. Customers' needs and desires change. Competitive products or services change. The economy, society, the family, and even individuals change. For this reason, your position can change, too. The original iPhone was an innovative, iconoclastic new product. The current iPhone, not so much. Facebook was once the new, "cool" network, and now it's seen as the Microsoft Windows of social media. At one point, marijuana was an illegal product that only druggies used; now, it's practically become a health food.

Measure not only whether your positioning is working in the competitive marketplace but measure how your competition is changing and how customer tastes and needs are changing as well. Things change, and so your positioning may need to change, too.

Be ready to reposition as necessary. Sometimes this can be in response to a threat, i.e., your product is no longer seen as innovative, and sometimes it can be in response to an opportunity, i.e., shifts in consumer preferences create new demand. As you measure what's working and what's not, keep in mind the distinction between "reality" and "perception." You can measure, succeed, or fail at both the level of the real product features and benefits and/or at the level of the perceived product features and benefits.

Chapter 5
Twaggle: Build Your Marketing Plan

As we come to the end of Section I, it's time to **twaggle**. It's time to use the think / do / measure methodology to build out the first parts of your **marketing plan**. Here are your to-dos:

1) **Write a Business Value Proposition**. What do you sell? Who wants it? Why?

2) **Identify your Buyer Personas**, including their demographic, psychographic, and situational characteristics. Organize people into "stereotypical" buyer personas and use these personas to look at your product or service from their perspective. Drill deeper into who wants your product or service. What are the characteristics, attributes, and/or situations that compel them to be "in the market" for what you offer?

3) **Define your brand**. What are the *skills* and the *attributes* of your brand? Are you a Tesla or a Chevy? An Aldi or a Trader Joe's? Don't try to be all things to all people. Once you have a clear handle on your brand, start thinking about *brandING,* that is, about how you are going to promote and nurture your brand among your target customers.

4) **Ponder your positioning**. We live in a competitive world. What's *unique* about your product or service? How does it stack up against the competition? If a customer asked you, "Hey. What do you have that the other guys do not?," what would be your answer?

The twaggle in all of this is to zig and zag between the "theory" of each of these elements and the "practice" of what actually works to build your brand and sell more stuff. You gotta start somewhere, but don't be afraid to revise these first elements of your marketing plan as you "learn from experience."

SECTION II
PROMOTION

At this point, you've written your BVP. You have a good idea of your buyer personas. You have a product or service with an educated guess (or practical experience, if you are an ongoing business) of the people who'll want it and why. You've even thought through your "brand" and your "branding strategy."

You're in great shape! Do you just sit back and wait for the dollars to roll in? Unfortunately not. Because just building a "better mousetrap" does not mean people will find out about your product or service, get excited about it, and beat a path to your door to buy it.

How, in short, do people find you? How (and why) do they get excited about you? How (and why) do they share the news of your incredible company with their business colleagues, friends, and family? In Section II, we'll dive deeply into the "Five Discovery Paths" so you can "fish where the fish are." This conceptual Section works *fishing-rod-to-fishing line* with Section III, "Deployment," where you'll turn concepts to action as you truly begin to fish for customers.

Chapter 6
The Customer Journey & the Sales Funnel

As marketers we can fall into the trap of thinking about marketing only from the perspective of our business, product, or service. That's important, but it's also important to look at everything from the **customer's perspective**. The *twaggle* is to get your marketing message across to the customer as they proceed along what has come to be called the "customer journey." Seen from the perspective of the company, this journey is called the "sales funnel." The customer journey and the sales funnel are opposites sides of the same coin.

Let's investigate.

THINK: the AIDA Model of the Customer Journey

"AIDA" is one of the most common ways to describe the customer journey. "AIDA" stands for "Awareness," "Interest," "Desire," and "Action." The AIDA model postulates that a customer goes from "awareness" (*they become aware that your company, product, or service exists*), to "interest" (*they begin to compare / contrast your brand against the competition and against their perceived needs or wants*), to "desire" (*they become positively oriented towards your brand*), to "action" (*they take the step of a purchase*).

Along the way, the customer learns about your brand, gets excited about your brand, and takes the final step of a purchase.. They **become aware of** your brand through advertising, word-of-mouth, and e-word-of-mouth, they **trust** your brand because of your online reputation as well as the views and reviews of friends or family, and they **purchase** your product or service via either an e-commerce interaction or a real-world transaction.

Let's take the example of *Jason's Cat Boarding Emporium*. We know what we offer ("cat boarding") and to whom we offer it ("busy San Franciscans with cats"). A typical "customer journey" would be as follows.

First, in the **awareness** phase, the potential customer or "prospect" becomes aware that he has a need for a place to stash the cat in preparation for a business trip or vacation. He is thus aware of a **need** or **desire**. He then becomes aware that there are services that he can hire to take care of his precious kitty, *Bubbles*. At this stage, he might begin to do research by searching Google or Yelp. Or he might reach out to friends and family on Facebook or in the real world for ideas or recommendations. Or he might see an ad for "cat boarding services" while reading his favorite blog or watching his favorite YouTube channel on everything feline.

Second, in the **interest** phase, he would identify a set of vendors who offer cat boarding services. He would explore their offerings and reputations. As he gets closer to a purchase, he might explore each potential vendor and research their reputations both online and offline via friends, family, and business colleagues. (Some models call this second phase, the "consideration" phase). For example, he might search Google for "reviews" of "Jason's Cat Boarding Emporium," visit our website or check us out on Instagram. These "trust indicators" would validate that we are an honest vendor with the services he offers. He might come in for a physical tour or call on the phone.

Third, in the **desire** phase, he would take steps towards making a purchase. He would narrow down his choices to just a few vendors, and he might take steps such as a free, no obligation facility tour or view YouTube videos of our facility online. He might interview vendors on the phone. Perhaps he might even use us, first, for a short trip, such as an overnight business trip. Then, once satisfied, he might use us for a longer stay.

The final or fourth phase is simple: he makes a purchase. If you look back across the journey, he has traveled from awareness to action or from prospect to customer. (Some models call this third phase the **conversion** phase). But it is important to note that marketing does not stop there.

Indeed, some models go beyond AIDA to identify post-purchase phases called "loyalty" or "advocacy." These refer to customers who love you so much they keep coming back or even adore your brand so very, very much that they write a review on Google or Yelp, take a selfie to Instagram of themselves with their kitty at the boarding center, or even create a TikTok showing just how much fun it is to board a cat at Jason's Cat Boarding Emporium. These customers are often called "advocates" or "superfans," and they are worth their weight in gold!

Now, let's look at the "customer journey" from the perspective of a marketer. The phrase used is "sales funnel." First, you create free content such as a webinar, white paper, or free consultation. You promote this content through SEO, advertising, or social media. I often call this the "carrot" as in "carrot" and "outreach marketing." Next, the customer becomes aware of your "carrot," that is, he or she becomes aware that you're offering a webinar on "cat boarding options" or have a free tool (available after registration) that analyzes your cat's personality and recommends in-home or away-from-home boarding options. Third, the customer goes through some back-and-forth with your website or company. They might browse the website and watch your videos on YouTube. They might call in and speak with a real person. They might come in for an in-person tour of Jason's Cat Boarding Emporium.

Finally, this "sales lead" becomes a "sale" at the bottom of the funnel. Seen in this way, you can see that the "sales funnel" is just the "customer journey" viewed from the perspective of the marketer.

DO: Promote Your Brand Along the Customer Journey and Sales Funnel

Your goal is to promote your brand in appropriate ways along the customer journey, and sales funnel. Your **to-do** is to map out each phase of the customer journey and do your utmost for your brand to be present and to be positively perceived at each phase. With that map in hand, your next **to-do** is to look at each stage (and any subordinate stages) and figure out the appropriate *messaging*, the appropriate *medium*, and the appropriate *mechanism* by which the customer will "see" your brand and "realize" it's compelling. Most importantly, brainstorm something "free" such as a "free" webinar, "free" ebook, or "free" no obligation consultation. Use this carrot in your outreach campaign. Everybody likes a free taste of the ice cream, for example. What's your "free sample" as relating to your product or service?

For *Jason's Cat Boarding Emporium*, perhaps we'll offer a free one-night stay, a free webinar on raising stress-free cats, or a free consultation on how best to accommodate your cat when you depart San Francisco on a business trip. Next, we might place ads on Facebook to generate brand awareness among cat lovers and ads on Google to generate the action of a click to the website. We would chart out answers to questions such as the following. Where will awareness advertising be placed? What will the message be? What will the desired next-step action be, and so on and so forth? How can we move potential customers along the "customer journey" or down the "sales funnel?"

Indeed, after a sale has been made, there might even be efforts to follow up face-to-face, by email, or even by telephone survey to ask customers to "do us a favor" and write a review on Google or Yelp. The *messaging*, the *medium*, and the *mechanism* by which we contact customers will vary based on where they are on the customer journey and what's most appropriate for our brand building.

Your **to-do** is to chart this out for your own business as well; the bigger and more complicated the brand, the more complex this map will be. The **twaggle** is that this isn't a straightforward process; the customer journey is more a zigzag than a straight line, and your brand identity is there at the beginning, middle, and end of your relationship to customers. It's always there, and it's always "being built" as opposed to "built" and "set in stone."

MEASURE: Where Does the Journey Break Down?

The final to-do is measurement. An easy way to do this is to move along the customer journey from awareness to interest, interest to desire, and desire to action. Measure the impact of your brand at each step.

First, does your initial brand identity capture the needs, hopes, and dreams of your target customers? The most defined brand identity isn't worth a hill of beans if it doesn't resonate with target customers. If they're aware but not buying, then you may have a malformed brand identity. Second, assuming your brand identity is solid, how much awareness is there? Measure how aware customers are of your brand; if there is no awareness, there can be no progression to the next steps. Third, is there interest in the brand up to and including a passionate group of superfans? Do people download your eBook? Sign up for your free consultation? Go crazy for your free webinar? Not every customer will be a superfan, but there should be at least some customers who passionately respond to your brand in a positive way. Where are they, and how many of them are there? Is your fan base growing?

Finally, is an action taken? The goal of marketing is to sell more stuff, and if they hesitate at the precipice of purchase, then something's wrong in the messaging. Are you getting leads? Are these converting to actual sales? If so, why? If not, why not? If you get an amazing brand response yet your sales are flat, debug what's wrong and figure out how to fix it. As we proceed in the next few chapters, we will pivot our perspective back towards the brand. But remember to look at each aspect not only from the perspective of your buyer personas but also from their location along the customer journey.

Chapter 7
The Five Discovery Paths

How do customers "**discover**" you? This is perhaps *the* most important question in marketing. Why? Because if a customer can't find you, if a customer doesn't learn about you, if a customer isn't jazzed about your brand, they can't buy your product or service. And if you don't have a firm grasp on how customers discover you, you don't know where to put your marketing efforts. You can't *fish for the fish when you don't know where the fish are.* You'll be advertising on billboards when they use Google. Or advertising on Google when they use Facebook. Or focusing on organic posts on Instagram when they use reviews on Yelp. Or doing the Internet when they're all in the real world. Or sending postcards through the US mail, or using the print Yellow Pages when you've been living in a cave for the last two decades and failed to realize that nearly everything (but not absolutely everything) is online.

In short, many businesses fail to understand *how customers find them (Question #1)* and *how they, as marketers, can influence how customers find them (Question #2)*. In this Chapter, we'll overview the five **discovery paths**. In subsequent Chapters, we'll dig into each discovery path in more detail.

THINK: The Five Discovery Paths

How might customers find you? Let us count the ways.

SEARCH. The **search** path occurs when the customer is "searching" for a company, product, or service. For example, a customer is hungry. He types "pizza" into Google or Yelp. He browses available restaurants, chooses one, and shows up to get pizza. He *searched* for pizza. He *found* pizza. He *bought* pizza. The search path is the province of **SEO** (Search Engine Optimization), largely on Google but also on sites such as Yelp or Amazon that work via "keywords" to help customers find stuff that they want. **Google Ads** advertising or advertising on key search engines like Amazon or Yelp (where appropriate) is also helpful on this path.

The search path exists in the "real world" as well. When a customer goes to a mall and looks at the kiosk map to find out which stores sell gifts, for example, that's the search path. Ditto for when she uses a directory of business accountants or when she asks friends or family if they "know any good painters." The key concept in **search** is that the customer knows what he wants, and he **pro-actively searches** for it.

TRUST. The trust path is based on "trust indicators." (Some marketers also call it "social validation"). In it, the customer already has created a list of vendors he might use, but he is researching "whom to trust." In this path, he might use the "reviews" and/or "stars" on Yelp or Google as "trust indicators" to predict which pizza restaurant is good (or bad). **Reviews** and **stars** are the most common trust indicators in social media marketing, but having a robust Facebook page with many followers and interesting posts can also be a "trust indicator." Having an expert-looking profile on LinkedIn can be a "trust indicator" for a CPA or an architect. A recommendation from a friend or colleague also plays into reviews and trust. The review / recommend / trust path is all about a customer "asking for help" from friends, family, business colleagues, or online review sites like Yelp, Amazon, TripAdvisor, etc. The key concept in review / recommend / trust is the reliance on *external validations* such as recommendations from friends or stars on Yelp.

SHARE. Wow! That pizza was great! Let me take a selfie of me chowing down on the pizza and post it to Instagram. Or, wow, here is a cat video of cats at the pizza restaurant puzzled by the self-serve soda fountain. It's "gone viral" on TikTok and has sixteen million views! Or, oh my goodness, Oprah has just recommended we read the novel, *An American Marriage,* by Tayari Jones, so let's buy it on Amazon and get started.

The **share path** occurs when a customer loves the product, service, or experience with enough passion to "share" it on social media – be that via electronic word of mouth (eWOM), a share on his or her Facebook page, a "selfie" on Instagram, or a viral video on YouTube. Others find out via shares from their friends or influencers, and suddenly yours is the most popular pizza joint in town. Indeed, **influencer marketing** is a type of marketing that straddles both the review / recommend / trust marketing and the share path; an "influencer" like Kim Kardashian recommends new jewelry, and then everyone goes out to buy it. The *influencer* is just a "trust indicator" *par excellence* with the push of *share* behind him or her.

In a sense, therefore, the "share" path is the flip side of the trust path. The key concept in share is when a customer or influencer pro-actively "pushes" her love of your product or service to friends, family, or business colleagues. The "share" path is more pro-active, and the review / recommend / trust path is more passive, but they are closely related.

INTERRUPT. The interrupt path is the bad boy of marketing, both online and off. It's what we think of when we say "advertising," but it's somewhat broader than that. Interrupt marketing occurs when you want to watch a YouTube video, but before you can watch it, you have to view an annoying ad. Or it's the ads on TV that we "must" watch (at least had to watch before TIVO and DVRs came along) before we see the live sports event we want to enjoy. Or, it's when you get a "cold call" or "spam email" from a recruiter who's viewed your profile on LinkedIn, or when you get a spam email on "amazing Viagra." Interrupt is largely **advertising** and largely advertising to "push" products that people aren't proactively looking for. But just because people hate it doesn't mean it isn't useful. Spam works, and so do TV ads.

BROWSE. The browse path is all about getting your message *adjacent* to what a person is reading or viewing. In it, you're looking for something, reading something, or watching something, and alongside comes something else. For example, you go to YouTube to look up "how to tie a tie," and in the suggested videos at the end might be a video for Dollar Shave Club. Or you might see Dollar Shave Club videos suggested at the right of the screen. You're not proactively looking for Dollar Shave Club, but you see their information as you "browse" for related content on sites like YouTube, Facebook, or blogs. Or, you go to the mall "to shop" and happen to wander into a boutique, only to buy the newest dog toy - something that you really hadn't been considering buying in the first place. Or you read a newspaper or journal or go to an industry trade show and just "happen" to notice a new product or service. The **browse path** is about getting your product or service *adjacent* to something the customer is looking at.

These are the five **discovery paths**, and as you look to your marketing, you'll see that everything in promotion can fit into one of these paths. There are both digital and non-digital examples of them. A door-to-door salesman, for example, is engaging in interrupt just as an unsolicited spam email or telemarketing call is, too. An ad on a billboard is "browse," just as an ad on the *New York Times* online is browse, too. Every promotional choice fits into one of the five discovery paths.

You'll also quickly realize that most marketing in the "real world" isn't pure. It has elements of more than one path. When you get an influencer to recommend your product, for example, you're using both the *share* path and the *review / recommend / trust* path. Or, when you use SEO to propel a blog post to the top of Google, you're using both the *search* path and the *browse* path to get your product or service in front of potential customers. They find an interesting blog post through a Google search, they read it, and then they discover your product or service "adjacent" to the post. The marketing or promotional mix will often seek to engage customers across a range of paths, but it's useful to see them as distinct discovery methodologies.

DO: Map Your Discovery Paths

We'll look at each path in more detail in the following Chapters, but for now, do a quick mental experiment by returning to your list of *buyer personas* and their position on the *customer journey*. Imagine you are each one of your buyer personas, and you have a possible interest in your product or service. How do you go about discovery? Is it largely search - you pro-actively go to Google or Bing to search for the product or service? Or is it more passive; you read reviews online or wait for family, friends, or business colleagues to recommend the product? Or, perhaps you aren't really pro-actively searching at all. Perhaps the customers passively wait for cues from influencers as to what to like and what to buy.

If a product or service is iconoclastic and completely innovative, then people don't know to look for it (*because they don't even know or understand they need it*). In that case, not only influencer or share marketing but interrupt marketing may be necessary. You may have to advertise in a pretty aggressive fashion to get the word out, or you may have to advertise or push your message first to influencers before you can reach customers. The great industrialist Henry Ford said, "If I had asked people what they wanted, they would have said faster horses." If your product or service is truly innovative, then people won't search for it because they don't know to look for it in the first place. You have to rely on interrupt or influencer marketing.

Here are the paths stated in question form. Your to-do is to research and answer each question.

Do your customers use **search**? If so, which search engines or other means of searching? Are your customers sensitive to **trust**? For example, do online reviews matter? Do influencers matter? Who or what influences whom? Is **sharing** appropriate? Who will, or at least might, share your product or service, and where are the influencers so influential that a few "mega sharers" can push consciousness of your product? Is your product or service so innovative, so new, that no one even knows to look for it? If so, what type of **interrupt** advertising should be used, and how can you make this cost-effective? Is your product or service naturally adjacent to some types of content and thus amenable to **browse** marketing? Do your target customers read certain blogs or newspapers, hang out on certain social media sites, or go to certain juncture points to consume information? If so, where? If so, how can you get your message adjacent to this information?

Your to-do is to figure out where the fish are, so you can "fish where the fish are." Each product or service is different, and some will favor one path over the others, but most often, it will be a mixture.

MEASURE: The Shifting Sands of Discovery

Nothing stays the same in the world of business. Consumer tastes change; your competitors introduce new products or services, and you might even decide to tweak your offerings or create entirely new products or services. New ways to reach customers come along, too, whether it's the rise of Google in the late 1990s, Facebook in the mid-2000s, the smartphone more recently, or - this just in - the crazy TikTok phase where it seems like every teenager is on the platform.

The "measure" component of discovery is to pay attention to the feedback between product and service, on the one hand, and discovery paths, on the other. For example, consider the history of jeans in America. First, the product was invented in 1871 by Jacob W. Davis and Levi Strauss as sturdy, inexpensive, and practical pants for miners during the California Gold Rush. Next, they slowly morphed into everyday wear in America and even a kind of "rebel without a cause" fashion statement against the orthodoxy of formal clothes. Then came "innovations" like bell-bottoms (*if you can call bell-bottoms an innovation!*) in the 1960s and "skinny jeans" in the 1990s. We have *spandex* to thank for that shift. Originally, the jeans were advertised via "word of mouth." Then it was print and TV. Today's it's online advertising and social media marketing.

So tastes shifted, competitive innovations came and went, new ways to inform consumers arose, and the entire marketing ecosystem around jeans changed. We used to shop for jeans in stores, now a lot of this shopping is done online. We used to rely more on friends and family for style cues; now, we watch the Kardashians 24/7. We used to learn about styles from TV, and we still do to some extent, but we're more and more influenced by Instagram feeds from stars like the Kardashians or Rihanna.

This dance of change is probably occurring in your industry right now. As you market your product, therefore, stay in "measure mode," realizing that discovery paths can change to reflect transformations in the underlying market. The measurement to-do is to measure which discovery paths are most effective and why and to be aware that the relative mix of discovery paths can change at any time.

Chapter 8
Trust

*C*an I trust you? That is, can I *trust* that your products or services are as fabulous as you claim, that they do what you say they do, that my experience will be nothing short of fantastic? *Trust indicators* are a discovery path that sits right on the border between *discovering* a product or service and *taking action* to actually purchase it. The most powerful trust indicator these days is online **reviews** on sites such as Yelp and Google, Amazon and Airbnb, Tripadvisor, Priceline, Avvo, Healthgrades, and so on and so forth. There seems to be a review site for every possible product or service out there!

But there are other important trust indicators such as a good-looking website, being published in prestigious blogs, getting awards or validations from key industry associations, or even having a vibrant YouTube channel or fantastic Facebook Page.

Trust indicators are all around us, so first, you need to understand what the "trust" path is all about, and second, you need to focus on how you - as a business - can influence your trust indicators in a positive direction. Note that I am not advocating *faking* trust (or *faking* reviews); I am advocating instead that you nurture real, positive trust indicators from real customers in a proactive fashion.

THINK: Trust Indicators are All Around Us

Trust indicators are a critical element to successful marketing. For example, you might think that you can "trust" that BMWs and Audis are great cars, which they probably are. But then you might not "trust" that Volkswagens are so great, given that company's recent scandal over SMOG test falsifications, or believe that United Airlines is a good airline given its own recent travel scandals, or be primed to accept that Wells Fargo employees can be trusted to advise you truthfully on financial products or services. Trust is hard to win, and easy to lose, and easy to lose quickly.

Take the example of a visit to the doctor. Can she be trusted? We trust that the "doctor" is the doctor she claims to be. That she understands cardiology and that she is competent to operate on our heart. How do we know? We look to external validations such as degrees in medicine, state licensing agencies, or the confirmation that she is a physician "in good standing" at the local hospital. Even the "white coat" that she wears, the diplomas of her education proudly displayed on the office wall, and her demeanor in the patient / physician relationship speak to trust. Online reviews on Yelp or HealthGrades factor into the equation of trust as well. But do we really know?

Our trust for her, you see, rests not on a hard foundation of fact but rather on a softer foundation of third-party validation. Why? The fancy word for this is *information asymmetry*. She (and the state government or the hospital) knows more about medicine and about her qualifications than we do. And she, along with the state government and hospital, is better positioned than we are to project this "positive brand image" to the outside world. We, as potential patients, are hardly competent to evaluate whether doctor "A" or doctor "B" can be trusted. So we look to third-party validations for trust. This *information asymmetry* drives the need for trust, drives the consumer's quest for trust, and drives the games people play around trust in the marketplace. Trust indicators, you see, are surrogates for surety, and they can be manipulated.

Bring this down a level to a local business. Can you "trust" that Jason's Cat Boarding Emporium is truly as great as Jason claims it is? After all, Jason   the owner   is rather biased in his claim that Jason's Cat Boarding Emporium offers an incredible cat boarding experience in San Francisco for truly discriminating cats and their owners. The claim ("we're awesome") is validated by the quest for external trust indicators. What are these? Well, first and foremost, they are customer reviews online. You Google "cat boarding San Francisco," and you see and read the reviews on Google (and perhaps on Yelp) of the various cat boarding establishments. Who has a lot of reviews? Who has just a few? Who has a lot of five-star reviews, and whose reviews are two stars? The same goes for our doctor in the example above. Does she have a lot of positive reviews on Yelp? On HealthGrades? On Google? Well, then perhaps she can be trusted.

Online reviews, in short, are the #1 trust indicator for most businesses outside of word-of-mouth. I would argue that #2 is a quick Google search for the vendor name plus the word "reviews," and #3 is whether the vendor has a good-looking website, active social channels, and generally positive "buzz" around their brand online. Either the prospective customer finds positive validation online about your business and buys from you, or they find negative reviews about your brand and decide to go elsewhere.

You never know the customers you don't get because your trustworthiness online isn't very good. Ponder that for a moment, as it's important:

You never know the sales you won't get because your brand is being slammed by bad reviews and reputation online.

Most businesses focus justifiably on their online reviews as the most important factor in the review / recommend / trust discovery path. But there are other trust indicators that you can worry about (and improve) as well. There's your website, for instance. Does it look good? Is it up-to-date? There's your Facebook Page. Do you have one? Do you post frequently? Do others comment and discuss you on Facebook? Do you have positive reviews on Facebook? In the real world, there are even manifestations of trust such as whether the restaurant is crowded on a Friday night ("must be good") or empty ("must not be very good"), whether the restrooms are clean ("must be a clean restaurant"), or whether the person who answers the phone speaks good English ("must be a high-class place"). Trust is part of your brand image, online and off, and trust indicators are how that brand image is broadcast into the minds of customers.

You, as the marketer, can, should, and must identify, monitor, and improve your trust indicators.

Common trust indicators are:

Online reviews on external sites like Google, Yelp, Amazon, etc. A good-looking website. Third-party endorsements such as blogs or influencers who validate you. Good-looking photos of key employees on LinkedIn; LinkedIn, blogging, or other activity by employees online. Influencers who both endorse and promote you to their fans and followers. Blog posts by your company or key employees on other sites. Social mentions by influencers on Twitter, Instagram, LinkedIn, etc. Robust social profiles with many followers and many posts on Twitter, Facebook, LinkedIn, etc. An active blog on your website. Industry awards or recognition; being "on" the New York Times bestseller list (or equivalent in your industry) or being a "Super Lawyer" on Superlawyers.com. Membership in key trade associations, state licenses, and other forms of industry validations. Educational credentials of key employees, such as graduation from prestigious universities. Participation in partnership, training, or certification programs such as being Google Ads certified, Audi certified, certified in HVAC by Trane, etc.

Intellectually speaking, therefore, when you come to the review / recommend / trust path, you're looking, first, to figure out the trust indicators that matter to your business and customers and, second, to influence them in a positive direction.

Don't miss the most important trust indicator of all when a friend, family member, or business colleague endorses a business via **word-of-mouth**. For example: *Have you seen the movie "American Beauty?" Well, it's my favorite movie of all time, and I highly recommend you see it. Or the best trade show for social media marketing? Well, I recommend Social Media Marketing World held each spring in San Diego.* A personal recommendation via word of mouth – of movies, books, products, or services - is the most powerful trust indicator, even if it is the most difficult one to influence. But online reviews on sites as diverse as Amazon, Yelp, or even Rotten Tomatoes take the real-world aspects of trust and create an alternative type of word of mouth, eWOM, or "electronic word of mouth." Remember that each of the five search paths while, conceptually distinct in theory, cross over into the others in the real world.

Ironically, in the online environment, we are very likely to believe the opinions of *strangers* in what is called "**stranger marketing**," whereas we are quite skeptical of strangers in the face-to-face world. **Superfans** and **Influencers** are yet another type of stranger marketing, in which the power of a celebrity is, a bit synthetically, conflated with the trust we feel for a family member, friend, or expert. A superfan is a customer who passionately loves your brand - so much so that they write a review on Google, the post an article to their blog, or they even make a YouTube or TikTok video explaining your product or service. An "influencer" has come to mean a person with a large online fan base (e.g., lots of followers on YouTube, TikTok, or Instagram) who is willing to promote products for a fee. Influencers take money; superfans do it for free. Both are examples of review / trust / share marketing at work.

While many businesses take their online trust indicators as simply given, as factors that they can't influence, this isn't necessarily so. The smart marketers are busy nurturing trust indicators behind the scenes.

It can be as simple as asking for reviews. For example, consider this interaction between pizza patron and waitress:

> *"Do you like our pizza?"*
>
> *"Yes."*

"Well, great! Could you do us a favor and write us a review on Yelp?"

"Sure."

Simply **asking** happy customers to write a review on Yelp, share their experience on the Airbnb website, or review your book on Amazon can work wonders to bolster the sheer number of reviews and tilt them in a positive direction. Many people won't write a review unless you ask them, but if you do ask them, they'll do it. The same goes for recommendations and endorsements on LinkedIn, or even influencer "shoutouts" on YouTube or Instagram. You don't ask; you don't get.

So ask. Or get your employees to ask. Each and every time you encounter a "happy camper."

Yet here's a problem, especially with online reviews and especially with online reviews of "non-fun" businesses like plumbers, accountants, divorce attorneys, and the like. The reality of online reviews is that outside of restaurants, bars, and other fun establishments, the most likely person to write a review is the "unhappy camper." If, for example, I get my toilet fixed by a plumber, I am not exactly likely to run to Yelp, or go to their Facebook page, take a selfie of myself on my newly repaired toilet and share it to Instagram, and otherwise broadcast a review of my awesome "toilet fixing experience." This is unlike, say, when I take my wife out to a nice Japanese dinner in San Francisco, where in I want to "show off" to the outside world and "virtue signal" that I'm a "good husband" by sharing a selfie of us eating expensive sushi in the city. Or perhaps by writing a review on Yelp of our restaurant experience celebrating our Disneyesque marriage and fantasy fiction love affair.

Unlike my restaurant experience, I am not very likely to want to broadcast to the world that my toilet is now repaired, and I can now "do my business" in efficient privacy. In short, only fun and/or prestige products or services are likely to spur *spontaneous* online reviews. With nothing to prompt reviews, the most likely reviews a "non-fun" business will garner online tend to be negative reviews from unhappy customers. This is yet another form of *information asymmetry* in trust online.

It gets worse. All of the official terms of service of the main review sites (e.g., Amazon, Google, Yelp, Airbnb) forbid you from even asking for reviews. So let's get this straight. Consumers rely heavily on reviews to identify businesses, the most likely person to write a review is the unhappy camper, and yet you as the business owner are not supposed to solicit positive reviews, even from real customers? Yes, that's correct.

Here's the trust equation for a fun business like a restaurant:

Provide great service. Rely on customers wanting to narcissistically broadcast their virtuous and awesome lifestyles by writing reviews and sharing to social media. Enjoy fabulous reviews. Watch your business grow and revenues soar.

And here's the trust equation for a non-fun business like a plumber:

Provide great service. Wait, passively, for customers to write reviews (which won't happen). Get reviews from the few crazy and/or unhappy customers. Watch your business shrink and revenues decline.

Yes, of course, in both cases you must work to provide an excellent product and excellent service. That's a no-brainer, and everyone in the company must foster a culture of excellence. But what's counterintuitive is that if you are in a non-fun business, even if you provide a quality product or service, you are likely to get no reviews or mainly bad reviews if you are passive.

In all cases, the smart marketers are proactive when it comes to trust indicators. They just have to be even more proactive if the business is in a non-fun industry like plumbing, accounting, or legal services.

You must pro-actively ask for reviews, even though to do so is generally a violation of the terms of service of all review sites (Amazon, Google, Yelp, Avvo, Airbnb, etc.). In short, you must violate the rules to win the game.

Conceptually, you must - on the one hand - ask "happy campers" to review you, but on the other hand, steer clear of being "busted" by the review police on Amazon, Yelp, etc. To be clear, I am not recommending fake reviews or paying for reviews. I am only advocating that you pro-actively ask "happy campers" to "do you a favor" and share their experience on review sites like Google or Yelp or to social sites like Facebook or Instagram.

Welcome to the world of trust online. No one said it was logical or fair. But the game can be won nonetheless.

DO: Identify and Nurture Your Trust Indicators

That trust indicators are important should be obvious by this point. But which trust indicators and where? If you're an attorney, these might be reviews on Google or on specialized sites like Avvo or Superlawyers.com, but also speaking engagements at local events, published articles in prestigious law journals, having a good-looking website, garnering prestigious awards or validations from key industry bodies, and so on and so forth. Even having an impressive-looking office for your law firm in a prestigious downtown neighborhood or wearing expensive Italian business suits are yet other types of trust indicators. If you've ever wondered why attorneys and politicians are among the last folks to wear suits and ties, it all comes down to trust. They're trying to project an image of trust because, ironically, they are among the least trusted members of society!

So to reverse that problem, you as an attorney or politician need to invest in good-looking suits and ties that convey to judge, jury, and potential client that you can be trusted. The abstract "trust indicator" gets translated into the concrete "buy a nice suit." Your **to-dos** for your business are, first, to identify which trust indicators matter to your target customers and, second, do what's ethically possible to get those trust indicators bent in a positive direction. If it's suits, buy a nice suit. If it's membership in key industry trade associations, join up. And if it's online reviews, get positive reviews online.

Let's say you have a Japanese restaurant in San Francisco; reviews on Yelp are thus critical. You need to politely and efficiently encourage and ask happy customers to review your restaurant on Yelp. It could be as simple as putting a "find us on Yelp" sticker in the window. Or educating each waiter or waitress to ask happy customers to please "review us on Yelp." Or it could be realizing that Google reviews matter, too, so using a service like "GatherUp" (**https://gatherup.com**) to pre-survey customers and then prompt the happy ones, and only the happy ones, to review you on Google. Then there's getting blogged about by food bloggers in San Francisco, the health department sticker with a grade of "Pass" in the window, and even making sure that the tables near the windows are stacked with customers on a Friday night. Inventory what encourages potential customers to "trust" that you are a good Japanese restaurant, and work on each trust factor one by one.

Or, if you're a plumber in San Francisco, you'll realize that your customers go online to Yelp and Google to find the best plumbers but are reluctant to review you after the fact. Your situation is like the Japanese restaurant, only more difficult because few people write positive reviews of plumbers spontaneously. In this contradictory way, the trust indicator of reviews matters even as the customers aren't very likely to participate. While you can't incentivize customers to write reviews, you can incentivize your plumbing staff. Perhaps you can pay "Bob the plumber" an additional $25 each time he garners a positive review on Yelp. Your to-do is to incentivize the employee but not the customer to encourage positive reviews. Or it could be an email survey sent out by the central office after each plumbing job.

Finally, in intellectual industries such as accounting or law, you'll want to work on your thought leadership. Being active on social media sites like LinkedIn, getting published in prestigious blogs, and giving talks at industry events even if these things are not read speak to your trustworthiness. Teaching a class at Stanford Continuing Studies, or having a book on Amazon with over five hundred reviews, is yet another way to bolster trust in a more professional or intellectual industry.

In short, your to-dos are #1 to identify which trust indicators matter to your business and #2 to create a systematic way of nurturing these indicators. Once you have strong trust indicators, then your #3 to-do is to showcase them. Perhaps you have a sign in the restaurant that says, "Check us out on Yelp; we now have 300 reviews," or you make sure that your website references your numerous positive reviews on Yelp. Or you showcase to your blog the recent attorney presentation at the State Bar Association of Nebraska. Or to the influencer on YouTube who used your shampoo – you make sure to showcase that celebrity endorsement on your shampoo packaging, and so on and so forth.

Once you've got trust, flaunt trust.

MEASURE: Are You Becoming Increasingly Trustworthy?

A boy scout is trustworthy, loyal, helpful, friendly, courteous, kind, obedient, thrifty, brave, clean, and reverent. But some are *more* trustworthy than others, and some are moving in the right direction, while others are moving in the wrong direction. So it goes for your own business. After you've identified the trust indicators that matter to your customers, the measure to-do is to quantify:

The number of trust indicators you have at the present time (e.g., how many reviews do you have on Yelp, Google, or Yellow Pages?). The sentiment of those trust indicators (i.e., is your star score a five, a four, or a three-point five, or are the reviews speaking in positive terms or more negative terms?). The visibility of your trust indicators (i.c., can customers easily find them and know about them?)

You want to measure whether you're getting more trust indicators, whether the sentiment is increasingly positive, and whether the visibility of your trust indicators is increasing. There's an added bonus when it comes to reviews, especially reviews on Google and Yelp. The number of reviews a local business has is a key factor in whether that business will rank high on Google, Yelp, and Bing (which uses Yelp reviews in its algorithm). The same goes for review-based sites such as Amazon, Avvo, Healthgrades, etc.

As you measure the trustworthiness of your business, ask customers not only "where did you find us?" but "what factors convinced you to give us a try?" Keep a constant lookout for new media that convey trust. Facebook reviews, for example, are a relatively new player in business trust. Once you know that local businesses can have reviews on Facebook, the to-dos become turning this feature on on Facebook and growing your Facebook trust. Pay attention and measure which methodologies are the easiest ways to grow trust. For example, is having the waiter ask a happy customer to review you on Yelp more efficient than sending a follow-up email? Is it more important to have reviews on Google or Yelp, BBB, or Yellow Pages? And if an attorney gives a presentation at a prestigious State Bar Association workshop, does anyone care? Learn what trust indicators exist, which ones matter in the minds of customers, and what is the most efficient process for nurturing a positive trust footprint. Measure your efforts at growing them, and measure whether all this positive trust builds your brand and helps you sell more stuff.

Chapter 9
Search

Because promoting your product or service is a critical part of marketing, it's worthwhile to really dig into each discovery path. The **search** path occurs when the customer is "searching" for your product or service. It's easy to see with "pizza." The customer is hungry. She goes to Google and types in "pizza." She reviews the results, clicks on your listing in the "Google local pack," and gets directions from her phone. She shows up at your restaurant and orders a slice. Her path goes from *search* to *purchase*. But it's more complicated than that; the devil is in the details.

THINK: the Details of Search

Search is the most proactive of the five discovery paths. The customer has an itch, and she intends to scratch it. Hunger begets pizza, pizza begets a search on Google, the search on Google begets a GPS map interaction on the phone, and entry to the restaurant begets a purchase. To think about the search path is to break it down into its elements, some of which are hidden and all of which are important.

Keywords. All search has "keywords" implicit within it. This is obvious on a Google search, but it's true even in a search on Amazon, Yelp, Avvo, Airbnb, etc., or in a directory or in a real-world interaction in which someone asks friends, family, or business colleagues for help. Dig into your keywords. Is it "pizza?" Or is it "Italian restaurant?" Is it "Pizza near me," or is it "best pizza in Chicago?" When we discuss SEO in Chapter 17, we'll return to keywords in detail, and I'll point out some nifty online tools for keyword discovery. But for now, realize that keywords drive search, and you - as the marketer - must really know your search keywords.

And it's not just about Google; it's about the semantic structure of how people look for stuff. When that customer asks friends, family, or business colleagues for help, does she ask them, "Hey, do you know a good *pizza restaurant?*," or is it, "Hey, we're having a casual office meeting, and do you know a good pizza restaurant that does *catering?*" Is the *catering* more important than the *pizza*, or the *pizza* more important than the *catering?* Pay attention to the word patterns or "keyword themes" that customers use to "discover" your product or service, and know them well — and in a very specific way.

Projection. Marketing is communication. Once you know the keywords that describe what the customer is looking for that matches what you offer, you have to project these keywords into every facet of your communication strategy. You can't offer catering at your pizza restaurant yet fail to mention that you offer catering on your signage, on your website, or on your menu. Customers aren't mind-readers, and neither is Google or Amazon!

Project your keywords into your signage (e.g., your sign on the street or your menu when they walk in), project them into your website (get them into the visible content, into the SEO-friendly HTML tags), project them into your product or service listings on sites like Amazon or Yelp, and project them into your advertising (your paid ads on Google,

Facebook or Yelp). Keywords help you to project that "you have" "what they want."

Location. Where does the search occur? Google comes quickly to mind in today's digital environment, but it's not only Google. For example, I work as an expert witness in litigation, and people search for me via the keyword phrase, *Google Ads expert witness*. They use Google, but they also use online directories such as Jurispro.com, so I optimize my profile on that directory for relevant keywords such as "Google Ads expert witness" or "Google Ads Expert." Indeed, in the real world, you might also have print directories that matter to your business, such as Chamber of Commerce directories or even trade show guides where you want to be correctly listed with your target keywords. Online there's Yelp and Amazon, Avvo and TripAdvisor, etc. Amazon in particular, deserves special mention. Amazon is a "search engine" just like Google; it's where people go to find stuff to buy. So if Amazon matters to you, what's your Amazon SEO and ad strategy? You need to not only know your *keywords* but also know *where* people are looking and make sure that those keywords are "in" your description. You have to "be" where they search, so figure out the location(s) where search occurs, both online and off.

Pizzazz. Yes, it's about keywords, and yes, it's about location. But it's also about **pizzazz**. Try a Google search for "pizza" or for "cat boarding in San Francisco" and look at the results that come back. Most will contain the target keyword, but how do you "get the click" from Google? It's not just about knowing the keyword, and it's not just about showing up high on the page. It's also about writing with sufficient pizzazz that it excites the customer enough to click from Google to your business. The same goes for a listing in an online directory, a listing on a review site like Yelp or Amazon, or even a listing in a print trade show guide.

Marketing is very much about brand image and pizzazz, so return to your Business Value Proposition and look to your brand attributes to help you write with pizzazz. It's competitive, so you must first know your keywords, second know the location where search occurs (and be noticeable there), and third have enough pizzazz to be the "sexy" choice, the "smart" choice, or the "right" choice.

DO: Identify Your Keywords and Where Search Occurs

The "do" component of the search path is to take what we've just learned and operationalize it for your business. Inventory the world "as if" you were a customer. First, brainstorm and research **which keywords customers use** and **where customers search for you**. Is it on Google? Or perhaps on LinkedIn? Amazon or Yelp? Avvo or Vitals.com? Is it in the real world, like you're a casual dining restaurant that is next to Interstate 80 in Grand Island, Nebraska, and they "search" for you by watching billboards? Or perhaps you sell in the B2B marketplace and what you sell is very esoteric and technical. So perhaps they search for you at your industry's annual trade show, or they search for you on the industry trade association website directory. Identify where the search occurs. Prioritize your marketing efforts to match the most important search venues that matter for your business.

To-do #1 is to identify the **keywords** that customers search for. Is it "accountant" or is it "accountant with expertise in international tax?" Or "CPA?" Or "tax service?" Is it just "lawnmower," or is it "commercial grade lawnmower?" Is it "pizza" or "casual catering services?" You need to know the keywords that match a customer's "pain point" or "desire." It can be something everyone needs ("pizza") or something that only a few people need ("ovarian cancer specialists in Baltimore"). And, as those two very different keywords imply, it can be something desired, or it can be a pain point. People generally either want to "get" pleasure or "flee" pain, so which is it? You must know your **keywords** in a very specific and systematic fashion. I recommend you build a keyword worksheet, which is a document that organizes your keywords into groups or families.

To-do #2 is to identify your search engines, both online and offline. Know specifically *where search occurs*. It's probably more than just Google. It might be Amazon, Yelp, Avvo, Airbnb, etc. Don't miss "specialized search engines" that are relevant to your business!

Your **to-do #3** has to do with messaging. Sketch out your **trust indicators, branding** and **pizzazz.** How do you not only get "in front" of the customer on the search path (e.g., rise to the top of Google, Amazon, Yelp, or Avvo), but also stand out with a positive brand identity? A good way to do this is to return to a buyer persona, pretend to be him or her, and do the actual searches for your product or service. Are you visible? Do you stand out? Do you look compelling, like the smart choice, the right choice, the sexy choice, or the fun choice? What do other competitors look like, and do you like how they present themselves? Inventory the competition and make a list of pros and cons of how they are not only findable but what their brand image is. Research your industry and competitors from keywords to where search occurs to the "pizzazz" that competitors project at the search locations. Position your company accordingly.

The **to-do #4** is to learn the rules of the search game. If you want to rank on Google, then you need to know the game is called search engine optimization (SEO), and you need to learn how to play it and win. (We'll discuss this in Chapter 17). Or, it might be learning and mastering the "game" of Google Ads, or perhaps ads on Amazon or Yelp. Or if you're an attorney, then it's contacting Justia.com or Abogado.com and making sure you have an easy-to-find, optimized listing. Wherever search occurs, there are games to play, rules to learn, and wins to be had. But you must learn how to win, so set that as your objective.

MEASURE: Search and Ye Shall Find

The "measure" component is to be open to new ways that search occurs, new keywords that your customers use, and even new twists or turns that speak to potential tweaks in your product or service, or even entirely new products or services. For example, to take Google as the most obvious search engine, you'd measure:

Your keywords. Have you identified the right keywords for your advertising or SEO?

Your rank. Do you actually show up on relevant Google searches? If so, where do you rank vis-à-vis the competition? (This might be important only on Google, or – if other search engines matter – it might matter on places like Amazon, Yelp, or even the directory at the mall).

Your performance. OK, you rank for a keyword. But do you get the click? If you get the click, does that click lead to a sale?

The measurement part of search is to compare the big search opportunities one to another, as in whether Google is more important to your business than Amazon, or whether a specific directory site like Avvo.com is more important than a competitor like Justia.com. Then within a specific search path, are you showing on the right keywords, are you getting clicks, and are those clicks converting? If it's a real world search path, the same rules apply, though the measurement of all this might be quite a bit more difficult.

Chapter 10
Share

Marketers often say that their best marketing channel is "word of mouth." That's certainly true, even in today's age of the Internet. When customer "A" tells customer "B" that your pizza is "fantastic," customer "B" is likely to both believe it (a "trust indicator") and head to your restaurant (a "form of promotion"). However, here's some good, new news: while *word of mouth* is hard to influence, *eWOM* – electronic word of mouth or, as it is sometimes called, "word of mouse" – *can* be influenced in a positive direction. The share discovery path is all about customer A (B, C, etc.) telling customers (D, E, F, etc.) about your product or service.

More exciting still are **superfans**; superfans are those customers who love your brand so much they write a review online, blog about you, post a video to Facebook or YouTube, etc. A variation here is **influencer marketing**, a specific subtype of share marketing wherein you attempt to get more popular or more powerful people to "talk up" your product or service to their followers. *Superfans* usually work for free or for "swag," while *influencers* usually want cold, hard cash. **Viral marketing** is when customers so intensely share your content that it reaches an exponential lift as influencers and superfans share to their followers, and their followers share it to friends, family, and business colleagues in an explosion of "buzz" across social media platforms.

THINK: What Gets Talked about, Shared, and Why?

What do customers share, and why? We're not talking about what they like as consumers or what they'd recommend if someone were to ask. We're talking about those situations in which a customer becomes a "brand ambassador" by *spontaneously* sharing information about a product or service *without* being prompted. Let's take movies, for example. On any given weekend, there is "the" movie that everyone wants to see or at least a list of three or four key movies that are new to theaters. Perhaps they've received sufficient buzz via advertising and influencers, or perhaps it's just that people look them up on Google by searching "movies near me," and Google happily provides a list of movies in nearby theaters.

More likely, customers rely on "trust indicators" as to which movies have good reviews from the critics or good reviews on review sites like IMDB (the Internet Movie Database) or Rotten Tomatoes. Perhaps they even ask a friend or family member what he thinks about movie such-and-such. These are all the paths by which a person with an interest in something to do on Saturday night becomes a "movie consumer."

But then, they go to see the movie. Perhaps it's the best picture winner for the current year, or perhaps it's the winner for the best-adapted screenplay. Or perhaps it's a totally new movie with few reviews and too early to have garnered an Academy Award. At any rate, a customer sees the movie. Here's where the marketing magic happens (or doesn't). They then show up at the water cooler at work and "share" their opinion of the movie. Maybe they tell a friend (or two, or three). Maybe they post to Facebook (or Instagram,

Twitter, TikTok). Or maybe not. The customer saw the movie, and he "loved it!" So he tells friends and colleagues, or perhaps she "hated it," and she tells them so. Or maybe the movie was so bland that they don't talk about it or share it at all. It dies the quiet death of marketing silence.

The same happens for the pizza restaurant down the street. The nail salon across town. The crockpot sold on Amazon that has a new auto-on feature. The smoothie recipe that burns fat and builds muscle. On and on and on for products, services, and brands across the economy. Some get talked about. A few get shared. And a tiny minority "go viral" and get so talked about, so shared, that they "go viral" until it's feeding frenzy of sales. Jay Baer and Daniel Lemin explore this in their fantastic book, *Talk Triggers* (**https://jm-seo.net/talk-triggers**).

Here's the question for marketers: why share? *Why* share the opinion and recommendation (positive or negative) at all? And why not just about movies but about the new local Greek restaurant or the new electric blender that comes with the new diet plan based on Ketogenic principles? The **share path** is something quite different from the search path, and as marketers, we want to understand it (and influence it in a positive direction).

Here you have to turn to social psychology. First, people are social animals. We evolved in hunter-gather social groups, and we evolved to earn social cachet by sharing information - there's a good watering hole over there, there are wild raspberries to be picked just around that hill, there's a predator lurking behind that cliff, or there's just some fun gossip about the higher-ups around the campfire. We "earn" social cachet by sharing useful information with others. By sharing the information on the wild raspberries (positive) or the predator (negative), we "help" our friends and family and thereby survive just a bit better than those hominids down the road that don't share. The information has to be useful; **utility** is one of the easiest "emotions" by which to grasp why things get shared. We share useful information with others, information that can "gain them pleasure" or help them "avoid pain."

Second, because people are social and emotional animals with a sense of justice, we also share **emotional** information. We share things that make us laugh or cry, and especially events or phenomena that go against our inner sense of moral justice. "Outrage" at the latest "moral transgression" is a big reason for sharing content, and among the emotions, "outrage" is perhaps the most powerful impetus to share. Notice how many shares on Twitter can be fitted into the phrase, "I can't believe he/she said that!" After outrage, humor - sharing something that is just plain funny – can also be an impetus to share. Sentimentality is yet another powerful sharing emotion, as when on Mothers' Day we share pictures of mothers with babies, or pictures of mothers with babies with puppies, or pictures of mothers with babies with puppies with an American flag, and so on and so forth. Anything that pulls at our heartstrings and makes us say to ourselves, "Aw shucks. That's so cute, beautiful, emotive…," well, that's something that has sentimentality pushing it along. **Emotions** are reason number two for sharing and are much more powerful than usefulness in the Internet age.

Finally, let's look at **narcissism**. We like to share things that make us look good, smart, better, benevolent, etc., things that put us in a positive light. We "virtue signal" to our peers about how moral, good-looking, affluent, and just generally superior we are to the "masses." When I share the fact that my wife and I went to the trendy new sushi restaurant in town - either via "real" word of mouth at the office water cooler, or via "e" word of mouth by sharing a photo to Instagram, or writing a review on Yelp, I am signaling to my friends, family, and tribe (and even my wife) that I am a "virtuous" person. I'm the guy who's a good husband, I'm the guy who has disposable income, and I'm the guy who knows where the new restaurant is in town and how to get a table on a Saturday night. This narcissistic or "virtue signaling" behavior is a key component in why people share.

I don't want to be a complete cynic here, but - in general - people don't share information for altruistic reasons. **They share to bolster their social position.**

With an understanding of the basics of why people share information, it's time to flip this around and brainstorm how you, as a marketer, can influence the basic human drive to share in a direction that helps your brand. First, identify what it is about your product or service that is **social**. Bathroom spray, for example, is something that's pretty private and rather embarrassing. So it's not something that we are likely to share via an Instagram photo or Facebook post spontaneously. A trip to Disneyland, my new Kawasaki jet ski, my new Lexus, a cruise to Mexico, or a trip to that proverbial new restaurant in town is something that is inherently social ("We do it with other people"), and something that positions us in a favorable light ("Look at me. I'm rich and happy.") These types of products or services are inherently shareable. So, first, figure out if your product is something inherently "fun" and "social" or something more inherently "serious" and "not social." If it's the former, then go to the next step. If it's the latter, you have to identify something adjacent to your product that has some share potential.

Returning to bathroom spray, which must be the least likely product to share on the planet, how would you go about creating a "share plan?" Look for **adjacent themes** such as the environment. Perhaps your bathroom spray is "green" or "eco-friendly" (built from organic or recycled ingredients, or using no environmentally harmful propellants), and perhaps by using it, a person is actually doing good by reducing consumer waste and saving the environment. Or perhaps your bathroom spray company only uses sustainably grown ingredients for the scents or sponsors various eco-friendly nonprofits. The marketing plan can attach the product, "bathroom spray," to the adjacent theme, "environmentalism," to provide some share power as people might want to "share" how they "support" the environment. Even better, you can attach the product to humor via a comedic video such as "Girls don't poop" (http://jmlinks.com/41w), a video that, as of this writing, has garnered over forty-two million (!) views on YouTube. The humor of the video (the "adjacent" theme) creates the share power to encourage eWOM.

Second, as you can see with the viral video, "Girls don't poop," you have to make it easy for folks to share your content. YouTube has built-in share mechanisms (share buttons, the ability to share to Facebook, Twitter, or LinkedIn), so a humorous video on YouTube, by its very structure, is easy to share. Social media, in general, is the mechanism for sharing in the digital age. A cruise line or a theme park like Disneyland can create photo spots and even photo contests to encourage customers to take photos and then share them. To see this in action, just go to Instagram (**https://www.instagram.com/**) and search for *#contests* to see literally thousands of contests being created by vendors and set to encourage sharing by consumers. The point is that sharability can be engineered and encouraged; it does not have to be left to its own devices.

Finally, let's talk for a moment about what "goes viral" and why. At a structural level, for a video, photo, or blog post to "go viral" means that each person who shares it shares it with at least two others. It has to accelerate at a geometric level, so the difference between something that just gets shared and something that goes viral is that the viral post grows exponentially. But it's not so simple. The viral post must generally leverage human emotion - *outrage* being the most common, *humor* perhaps third or fourth in line, *usefulness* last on the list - and this creates potential problems for brands. Few brands want to be attached to anything other than a positive emotion, leaving humor to be the most common viral emotion for corporate messaging. Outrage, you see, while very powerful as a mechanism for sharing, can backfire against the brand. It can be done. But it's difficult.

Next, beyond the most common emotions for viral promotion on the Internet (outrage or humor), **superfan marketing** and/or **influencer marketing** is usually needed for anything to "go viral." Superfans – remember - are those who love your brand and will share "for free," while influencers usually want cold, hard cash. Your superfans and/or influencers talk about your video (photo, blog post, etc.) and share it, first, and then their followers hopefully share it, second. Behind the scenes, superfan marketing, influencer marketing, and even paid advertising are critical to the ignition of viral content on the Internet. It's not easy to "go viral," but that shouldn't deflect us from the value of shareable content. For superfan / influencer marketing to work, you have to a) identify the superfans / influencers in your industry, b) reach out to them and get their attention, c) convince them that there's "something in it for them" to talk about your brand, and d) get them actually to do it.

In most cases, superfans or influencers like to talk about products or services that improve their own social cachet. They participate in the "outrage waves" moving across Twitter, for example, to "virtue signal" that they are morally superior to whatever person or group committed the "no-no" against which we should all be outraged. Or they share photos of themselves using a product or service that makes them look cool, smart, or sexy to "signal" that they are the cognoscenti when it comes to knowing the next new thing.

And then there's **negative virality**. This is usually, but not always, a video against a brand, or a video that conveys shocking or outrageous information such as when United Airlines forcibly removed a passenger from a flight and the video "went viral," or when United negligently stuffed a dog into the overhead bin during a flight, or when United broke guitars. Just go to YouTube and type in "United Airlines" and follow the suggested searches of "United Airlines Breaks Guitars," "United Airlines Dog Dies," and "United Airlines Drags Man off of Plane," to see the epic social media sharing fails of one of America's largest corporations. (*It seems like United Airlines is a great business to look to for how "not" to do social media marketing*).

Businesses both large and small are on notice that they are "being watched," and even an innocent slip-up can "go viral," not to mention something truly outrageous and shocking as United Airlines seems to engage in with depressing regularity. All we can do as marketers is to educate each and every front-line employee that they must be on their best behavior and treat every customer with the politeness and respect that they deserve, even if they don't deserve it, because everything and everyone is being recorded in the digital era. **Outrage** against a **big brand** is a powerful catalyst for a negative viral event.

In short, to understand the share path in today's marketing is to understand the emotional causes and structural mechanisms that make it both desirable and possible, for a consumer to share content. Your job is to catalyze the positive shares around your brand and do everything in your power to mitigate the opportunity for negative shares, and clean up any mess that might occur.

DO: Encourage Sharing around Your Brand

Promotion is one of the key tasks for you as a marketer, so you obviously need to do everything in your power to promote your company, especially things that are free. Nothing is better in today's "share economy" than the spontaneous word-of-mouth and eWOM that occurs largely on social media. Your **to-do** then is to identify sharing opportunities that will help your brand in a systematic way. First, map out whether you have a "fun" product that lends itself easily to sharing (like a restaurant or a theme park) or a "non fun" product that does not lend itself so easily to sharing (like an accounting practice or an herbal medication).

Whether you are fun or not fun, look not only at the product or service but at **adjacent themes**. If you're a theme park, for example, realize that people are there "on vacation" and will want to share photos with their friends and family just for the sheer joy of sharing fun with "the tribe" but also to virtue signal that they're a happy family, having a fun vacation. If you're old enough to remember cameras and film, you may recall that Disneyland used to have markers of "good places to take a photo" that were designated as "Kodak moments" (which is where the phrase "Kodak moment" entered the lexicon). So your marketing to-do is to identify ways to nudge consumers to take that photo and share it.

If you're in a "not fun" industry, it's all the more important to look for adjacent themes. Aeromexico, for example, doesn't encourage the sharing of pictures of its airplanes, lavatories, or crowded seating arrangements, for example. Instead, it encourages the photo-sharing of the fun and historic destinations in Mexico to which it flies. The to-do is to find adjacent themes that are "share-friendly" and write those down in your plan.

Now that you've figured out whether you're a fun company in a fun industry, a not fun company adjacent to a fun industry, or (God help you), a not fun company adjacent to nothing fun, your second to-do is to inventory the available emotions. For most businesses, the emotional reasons will either be the "virtue signaling" that people do in a narcissistic fashion ("Look at us having a fun family vacation in Disneyland") or the emotion of humor. Go to YouTube and search for "Super Bowl commercials," and you'll see that many of them focus on a humorous theme to encourage social buzz.

Another good emotion is sentimentality. Whether it's Mother's Day or Valentine's Day, another emotional hook is "aw shucks, I agree." Many of us will positively respond to the "sentimentality" of these holidays and share content (photos, posts, quotes, blog posts, etc.) that signals our virtuous endorsement of the theme. Finally, for some nonprofits and a few businesses, the emotion of outrage can be leveraged as well. Your **to-do #2**, therefore, is to inventory available emotional themes and map out which emotions are both most likely to be shared in your industry and most likely to help your brand.

Third, you want to make efforts to encourage social sharing pro-actively. It can be as simple as posting a picture of a mother and child on Mother's day to Facebook and asking in the post for folks to share their memories of Mom. Simply asking folks to share is a basic method to encourage sharing, assuming that what's "in" the message fits into an emotional reason for sharing in the first place. Or it can be a little more complex as when Disneyland designates certain places in the park as "great for photos," knowing full well that half the population will share these photos to Instagram, Snapchat, or Facebook and thus implicitly promote the park. Or even more complex, it can be setting up a contest on Instagram or Facebook to choose the most photogenic birthday party at your pizza joint. You'll notice that much of shareable content "lives" in the domain of images and video, the reason being that visual content conveys emotions more quickly and easily than does the written word. Almost everything that "goes viral" is a video or image, for example, and not text.

The "Do" task when it comes to sharing thus breaks down into a) what **attributes** of your product or service are **shareable** (or, if not, what adjacent things can you work with), b) which **emotions** are most likely to encourage sharing, and c) **what can you do**, pro-actively, to encourage your customers to "spontaneously" (in quotes) share your message?

MEASURE: What Gets Shared, Why, and How Does it Help Your Brand?

The twaggle in sharing is to research what gets shared and why in your industry or adjacent themes, on the one hand, and to conceptualize whether it helps, hurts, or is neutral to your brand, on the other. Measure whether anything is being shared about your brand at all, and figure out why. Even a few spontaneous shares can be a goldmine for brainstorming. They're like weeds that have pushed their way out of the dirt. Imagine what can happen if you nurture, feed, and love them?

Next, as you pro-actively encourage sharing, look to measure your sharing inputs and any outputs that result. How many likes did a specific post garner on Facebook or Instagram? How many comments? And how many shares? Interactivity is where it's "at" on social media, and it's the foundation of sharability.

More specifically, so they're sharing photos of your restaurant, is it really helping you? Could you perhaps create a more proactive online "contest" or "challenge" around what's already shareable? Or, you realize that your brand of, say, a Mexican restaurant is adjacent to a fun theme, the Cinco de Mayo holiday. People, you learn, flock to the restaurant on that day, whether Mexican or not, to enjoy your great food and fun atmosphere. You've learned that there's an adjacent event, so the to-do is to leverage that event to encourage sharing. Perhaps it's a blog contest for your Facebook fans about their Mexican heritage and what it means to be Mexican-American. Or perhaps it's just a more fun photo contest in the restaurant of who looks the sexiest in a sombrero. But then you twaggle from this real-world event, "Cinco de Mayo," to realize that there are other holidays - Easter, 4th of July, Labor Day, Mother's Day, Juneteenth, Diwali - etc., that can be useful themes for social media content and that also have a built-in shareability.

Measuring helps you to see the specific reasons why content is being shared in your industry and to abstract from that to see more opportunities for sharing. Once you realize that Cinco de Mayo helps you, it's just a Google search away to identify other holidays that help sell Mexican food. Super Bowl and guacamole, anyone?

What gets shared and why isn't self-evident or stable. So the measure component is to research and leverage three components - attributes of your product or service, the emotions that motivate sharing, and the techniques and tactics you can deploy to encourage more sharing. And don't forget to monitor and measure any "negative sharing" that might be occurring around your brand, such as negative reviews on Yelp, hostile commentary on Instagram, or epic fails on YouTube. Research and learn from that, too, and then take steps to make negative sharing less likely.

Chapter 11
Interrupt

Interrupt marketing is what it says it is: *interruption. Stop doing what you're doing, and pay attention to me* — that's the message of a commercial during a televised sporting event, an unsolicited email that forces its way into your Gmail or Outlook, or the dreaded telemarketing call that comes during dinner. Ditto for ads on YouTube, Snapchat, or TikTok. Robocalls are the latest practically Satanic version of interruption deployed for marketing purposes. Interrupt advertising is often what people think of when they think "marketing," but as we have seen, it's just one discovery path among the five. As *consumers,* we hate interrupt advertising, so why, as *marketers,* might we even use it at all?

THINK: Why Interrupt?

Let's backtrack for a moment and review the other marketing paths. You'll see that, especially with respect to *search* and *share,* the consumer isn't avoiding the message. On the contrary, he's receptive to it. Take the search path, for example. When I am pro-actively searching Google for "cat boarding establishments in San Francisco," I am looking for a service that meets a need I already have. I know what I want, I am searching for it, and I am more than happy to click on an ad or organic result on Google or Yelp. I am in "search mode." This is why, not surprisingly, the return on investment for search-related marketing activities is generally many factors higher than the return on investment from interrupt advertising. People are primed to hear what you want to say.

Or, consider the eWOM / share path. Here, again, the consumer is pretty receptive to the message. Customer "A" has experienced the top quality service and amazing commitment to luxury of Jason's Cat Boarding Emporium, and she's more than willing to write a review on Yelp or share an Instagram photo of her and her happy kitty after a week of luxury at the Emporium. And her friend, Customer "B," well, he's also interested- first, because he personally knows Customer "A," and second, because he, too, has a luxury-minded cat and cats are just fun to look at on the Internet. He's not as primed for the message as in search, but he's not opposed to it, either.

But search and share don't always work. Why not?

First and foremost, they don't work for products or services that customers are not pro-actively looking for. When the original ShamWow! product came out, for example, no one "knew" that they needed a "ShamWow!" shammy, nor that the ShamWow! was more absorbent than paper towels, that it could pick up twelve times its weight in liquid, and so on and so forth. This "amazing" product was marketed by a sort of huckster-ish "As Seen on TV" type of marketing that was literally forced in front of you through push TV and Internet advertising. You didn't know that you needed it, so you wouldn't be searching for it. Indeed, so few people were using it, and the product isn't exactly photogenic, that the share path wasn't strong enough to push the marketing forward either. So interrupt marketing was the only available path.

Interrupt, in short, is used when the customer doesn't know he "needs" your product or service, he isn't receptive to recommendations or shares by others, or the enthusiasm for either search or share just isn't sufficient to make the marketing mix work.

There are more complex reasons as well why marketers might need interrupt in their toolbox. Let's dig deeper into solar panels as an example. Solar panels actually do work, people actually do need them, and a few people actually do search for them or recommend them to friends and family. So why might a solar panel manufacturer or installation company engage in the dirty game of interrupt advertising? Why is interrupt so common if it isn't generally as effective as the other paths?

Reason #1: stupidity. Some marketers are just plain stupid. They don't realize that a better use of resources would be search engine optimization or working to encourage happy customers to share their love and pride about their new solar panels. It's easy to buy obnoxious ads on YouTube or hire a robocall telemarketing service to blast call after call after call out, and who cares if you annoy a non-customer? Not to mention going to the dark side and purchasing a spam email list. Stupidity, in combination with laziness and a lack of ethics, can lead marketers to deploy interrupt tactics even when other tactics are available and might yield better results. A lack of metrics, a failure to measure whether things really work or not, is a contributing factor here.

Reason #2: acceleration. Another reason is to accelerate sales or brand awareness in a new market. Yes, there are a few core people who know what solar panels are and know that they want them and thus use the search path. And there are a few geeks who are so excited about solar energy that they share their love to Facebook, LinkedIn, Instagram, and the blogosphere. But they're not sufficient. It's not enough. So the marketer chooses or must choose the interrupt path. When a product or industry is new or immature, there just might not be enough energy behind search or share to achieve the desired sales results.

Reason #3: cost. Sadly, the costs of spam emails and robocalls have fallen so low that unscrupulous marketers can use spam email and robocalls to bombard one thousand customers to find that one customer who actually *does* want solar panels or actually *is* interested in tax incentives to install renewable energy on his rooftop. The same goes for the completely fake scams like the IRS is calling you because you owe back taxes, or a Nigerian Prince would like your help collecting his one million dollars, or this is "Kate from Google" with important information on your Google listing. The costs are so low to spam and robocalls that annoying a thousand, or even a million, people to reach the one person who is interested or easily fooled is "worth it," ethics be damned.

Reason #4: Branding. There is a final reason why companies use interrupt marketing, and this is to stay top of mind with their brand. Big brands, especially the big car brands and big beer brands, use a lot of paid advertising to "push" their message to us, whether we like it or not. The ubiquitous car commercials on TV, including on Super Bowl Sunday, are a case in point. Chevy, Dodge, GMC, and other big car and truck manufacturers hope that by bombarding us with unsolicited "interrupt" TV commercials, they can pound their brand into our head so that when I say, "Truck," you say, "Chevy." (*See, it worked*). You may not be in the mood today, to go out and search for a car or truck, but you have been subliminally conditioned through heavy advertising to recognize the major brands and even think that you are a "Chevy" person or a "Dodge" person.

Your soul was purchased through a billion-dollar interrupt ad spend.

Mix it Up. And, just to add another twist to the marketing screw, interrupt marketing can be used in combination with other forms. For example, you could use "interrupt" marketing such as unsolicited emails, phone calls, or even tweets to influencers to "get their attention" in the hopes that they will learn about your product or service and then share it with their followers. Or look at the phenomenon of Super Bowl commercials anew. The advertisers use interrupt advertising to get the ads seen by millions and then hope that the clever messaging is enough to spark a share phenomenon so powerful that the ads "go viral." It's not *interrupt* **OR** *share*. It's *interrupt* **AND** *share*.

Finally, don't fall into the mistake that *all* forms of advertising are *interrupt* in nature. That's not true. A search ad on Google is leveraging *search*, as you're searching for a product or service. A browse ad on Facebook is leveraging *browse* or *share*, and participation in a real-world trade show or a hosted webinar isn't necessarily about interruption. Advertising simply means *paying to get your message out*, and that message may be via search, via share, via browse, or via interrupt. Don't conflate advertising with interrupt, even though much of advertising is interrupt, and the bad name that advertising gets is entirely because of the dynamic of interrupt. Forcing us to watch your stupid commercial on

YouTube before we see that cat video we really want to see is a dangerous game that may make us hate you, after all. And all the forcing that goes on via interrupt is why advertising, itself, has a negative connotation. But not all advertising is interrupt, and not all advertising is annoying to customers.

On the other hand, not all interrupt is advertising either. Spam emails, or unsolicited emails in general, are a form of interrupt. Unsolicited tweets to a Twitter account or unsolicited outreach on LinkedIn, while organic, are also a type of interrupt. So are "cold calls," whether done by a real person or a robot. Door-to-door salesmen are a type of interrupt, as is any type of "cold calling" or "cold lead getting." Interrupt merely means that you as the marketer are forcing your way into a conversation with a potential customer. They are not looking for your product or service. They are not seeing it via a "share" from a friend or colleague. They are busy doing whatever they are doing and you are "interrupting" them with a spam email, a cold phone call, or an ad on YouTube.

DO: Shall You Interrupt?

The "do" component of interrupt marketing is something you can work out by stages. Your first **to-do** is to research whether your product or service needs the interrupt path. Is your product or service something so new or unusual that few people will pro-actively search for it? Or, is it so boring and non-emotional that few people will share their positive experiences with others? Is it really iconoclastic with no adjacent competitors or categories? Evaluate your product or service truthfully, and determine whether you need interrupt because of the product or service itself. Don't just use interrupt because you're lazy as a marketer.

Write down the pros and cons of each available path, including but not limited to interrupt. Remember that of all the five search paths, interrupt is the one most likely to backfire and create angry customers who really hate you. Being hated is not a good thing.

To-do #2 is to identify the best venues. Where do your customers "hang out?" Is it on TV, on YouTube, or perhaps LinkedIn, which offers unsolicited emails under the euphemism of "Message Ads?" If you are B2B and your target customers live via email, then unsolicited emails or InMails, as LinkedIn calls them, might be a good option. Or, if influencers are key in your niche, then a combination of using interrupt techniques to get the attention of the influencers, first, and, second, having something so cool they really do want to share it, might be a key part of your influencer marketing strategy. Did you know you can tweet to practically anyone? Well, those "unsolicited tweets" are a form of interrupt marketing. They may be necessary if the other paths won't work. Used wisely, interrupt marketing can work. Just choose your targets and venues with precision.

Your third **to-do** is to focus on your message. While you can buy interrupt ads easily on YouTube, that doesn't tell you what the content of your video ads should be. While you can buy "Message Ads" on LinkedIn, that doesn't tell you what the content of your email message should be. Tailor your message towards the emotional or practical desires, needs, or pain points of your audience. The ShamWow! commercials, for example, used a blend of campy humor mixed with an amazing (!) sense of the utility of the product. Your to-do here is to brainstorm the message in your ad or other media construct. Once you've got their attention, what message will they see, listen to, interact with?

At launch, then, you'll have defined the target media where your customers hang out and a message that fits their psychology. Don't forget to think of the fourth **to-do**, which is the offer itself. If you're going to interrupt someone and basically shout to get their attention, you need to offer something amazing, preferably free for starters. It's usually better to offer something soft and non-threatening like a free webinar or eBook than to go for the jugular and yell at them to "buy now" before it's "too late." Even the Nigerian Prince who sends unsolicited emails tries to build rapport before tricking you into giving him your bank information. Sketching out the desired steps to be taken after the "unsolicited" message is seen, listened to, or interacted with is **to-do** #4.

MEASURE: We Interrupt This Broadcast to Learn Whether Any of This is Working

Because interrupt is obnoxious and because the costs tend to be high, interrupt is the last marketing method you should "put out there" and not measure. Measurement is key. Is your interrupt campaign working? And, more specifically, what's working about it, what's not, and what can you do to improve it? You want to twaggle between the specific steps you are implementing, such as building a list of email or phone contacts to send unsolicited communications to and the results that occur. Do people "take your call" or "click on your email?" If so, do they listen to the message, and then do they take your desired action?

Don't build a wall between the telemarketers on the front lines and you, as the marketer, in the command post. Did it work? What did you learn? How can you tweak it to be better? Measure it step-by-step:

Targeting. Are the right people receiving your message? If not, can you do a better job of identifying who is likely to be receptive and taking out from your targeting the people who are not?

Messaging. Is the message the right one? Which emotions, desires, utility, or other factors are the core of the message, and are they gaining traction? Why or why not? Because interrupt is a brute force method into the customer's consciousness, those initial few seconds are key. Is the "hook" working to get them to agree to listen to the rest of the message? Do they immediately hang up on your call or skip past your YouTube video ad? Why or why not?

Desired Action. Are the prospects taking the desired action? If it's an unsolicited telemarketing campaign, are they not only taking the call but at the end of it agreeing to the next step, such as attending a free Webinar or accepting a free eBook? Are they clicking from your YouTube ad to your website? If the action is too scary, scale it back to something less threatening.

The measurement process here is to toggle constantly, or I would prefer *twaggle*, between the conceptual structures and goals of your interrupt marketing efforts and the real-world results. Be on the lookout for new opportunities for better targeting, better messaging, and better next steps. Be on the lookout for new opportunities for interrupt marketing, such as new ad formats on Google, Yelp, Facebook, Twitter, YouTube, etc. Ironically, interrupt is the *easiest* type of marketing to set up because most of it (though not all) is paid advertising. Yet, it is the *hardest* type of marketing to get to succeed. There's even a saying, "Advertising is like sex. Only losers pay." That's a bit harsh, but the point not to make interrupt advertising the only tool in your toolbox is well taken.

Chapter 12
Browse

T he "browse" path simply means that the customer "discovers" your product or service when they are looking for something else. In the real world, it can be as simple as when shoppers shop in a mall, browsing from store to store or from rack to rack only to "discover" something new that they want to purchase. Or at the grocery store, when they're browsing for diapers and "discover" fragrance-free, eco-friendly baby wipes made from organic bamboo conveniently placed nearby. Browse is your signage in the mall, the "place" your product is discovered and what it's "next to," and even your listing on the mall kiosk. It is billboards on a highway, and – online – it's ads placed next to articles on CNN and even guest posts in blogs. *Browse* is getting your message *adjacent* to what they're looking at.

THINK: The Adjacent Science of Browse

The word "browse" comes from a late Middle English word from the French, *broz*, which comes from "shoots" or "buds." The idea is as cattle graze for food in a field, they are "browsing" for leaves or plants and thus "coming across" new things to eat. In this way, it's entered the lexicon as a term for shopping as when a salesperson comes up to you and asks, "Can I help you find what you are looking for?" and you just answer, "I'm just browsing." Notice how in this very common interaction in a store you have, implicitly, two different discovery paths: *search* (the salesperson is asking you if you need help finding what you are searching for) and *browse* (no, you're just looking here and there, not sure exactly what you have in mind, or even if you want to purchase at all).

Words give clues to deeper marketing meanings.

As is often true in marketing, you should flip this concept around in your mind. If customers often "browse," then how do you get your product or service "next to" the things that they are looking at? Browse in retail is the struggle for "product placement." The struggle to get your product placed at eye-level and the struggle to get your product placed in the right category and adjacent to complementary categories. Peanut butter is next to jelly in the supermarket, and that's by design, not accident. Marketers compete to get their peanut butter or their jelly into the most visible spot.

Online the struggle for browse is also about categories and adjacency as well. Take Amazon.com. We often go to Amazon starting with a *search* intent, such as searching for "books on WordPress," and then "browsing" the Amazon search results and suggestions, looking for related books. Amazon even encourages this type of online browsing with its "Customers who bought this item also bought" feature that is shown beneath each product page. Or, after you make a purchase, Amazon will send you a push email explaining, "Based on your recent visit, we thought you might be interested in these items," thus combining "interrupt" with "browse." Amazon wants to help you – the marketer – to get more sales by gently nudging the customer with browse suggestions.

Your job on the browse path, to continue the Amazon example, is to optimize your product listing so that the

Amazon algorithm can easily figure out what's adjacent or similar to your offering. Keywords in the product listing are paramount, as is the title of the book or product, and then there's sales behavior. Amazon figures out that a customer who buys "A" also buys "B," and this insight leads Amazon to suggest product "B" to the next customer who buys "A."

Or take browse and the blogosphere. Remember that when we discussed keywords in Chapter 9 on search engine optimization, we learned that there are "educational" or "early stage" keywords, and there are "transactional" or "late stage" keywords. If search is focused on "late stage" keywords, browse if focused on "early stage" or "educational" keywords. Browse is focused on getting your marketing message adjacent to customers as they "browse" to "learn more" about this or that topic.

For example, someone who has an aching pain might search Google for "causes of knee pain" or "treatments for knee pain," which are early-stage or educational searches. He then lands on a blog post that discusses common causes of knee pain, and adjacent to the blog post discovers advertisements for knee pain therapies. The ads are "adjacent" to the blog articles, and so the path for these ads (placed via what Google calls the *Google Display Network*) isn't search but browse. Ads on blogs, ads in the *New York Times* or your local newspaper online, and even ads on Gmail are really all about browse. You, as the marketer have to identify the most logical media placement and most logical keyword themes that are adjacent to your product or service and then place ads accordingly.

Ads on social media are often browse-oriented as well. If our sufferer from knee pain goes to Facebook, he can be targeted as a runner and shown ads on running products, including those for knee pain (a common affliction of runners). He's not pro-actively searching at this point; he's browsing Facebook for family and friends and perhaps information from his running pals. It's like the *interrupt* path in that Facebook ads get in the way of his browsing, but it's not nearly as obnoxious as a spam email, an unstoppable ad on YouTube, or a cold call. And, to return to the blogosphere, if he reads an article on a running blog on knee injuries written by your CEO (and strategically placed there by you), he can be marketed to without his really even knowing.

The browse path is about **adjacency**, about getting your message next to what the person is looking at, reading, or listening to. At a conceptual level, therefore, you must figure out a) where the customers are browsing (i.e., which media and what types of podcasts, videos, or articles), b) how to get your marketing message adjacent to relevant content, either paid or organic, and c) how to structure your article, ad, or "product placement" with a "hook" so compelling that the consumer becomes interested enough to click over to your website. If it's in the real world, as in product placement on a grocery store shelf, then it's unusual and interest-provoking product packaging that does the work. There's a bit of a *hijack* in browse, as you want them to stop "browsing" aimlessly and start "looking" more intently at what you have to offer.

To use *Jason's Cat Boarding Emporium* as an example, here's how we could build out a browse marketing campaign. We'd take the fact that people who need cat boarding are, obviously, cat lovers. We'd go to the Internet and identify the key blogs and bloggers that talk about cat care. We'd either reach out to them to "guest blog" on their blogs to share our insights on how best to board a cat without emotional disruption, or we'd advertise on these key blogs. In the real world, we'd take advantage of our position on a busy San Francisco street to have an unusual and eye-stopping sign announcing our services.

We'd offer low-priced or perhaps even free cat carriers with our unusual logo and hot color scheme to attract attention. We'd get our novelty cat toys and cat products into San Francisco's most prestigious pet stores, and we'd submit articles to the *San Francisco Chronicle* and other local papers about how San Francisco has the dubious distinction of having more pets than children in its population. Returning online, we might leverage Facebook advertising (via demographic targeting or the so-called "Facebook Pixel" for remarketing on the network) to target potential San Francisco cat lovers who are checking out Facebook. They'd be browsing Facebook for Facebook's sake, yet they'd see our ads and our posts adjacently touting the importance of stashing the cat at San Francisco's preeminent luxury boarding establishment for felines. Throughout, our objective would be to get our marketing message "adjacent" to every media opportunity where cat lovers consume content.

DO: Find Browse Targets

Your **to-dos** for browse follow this logic. First, you have to identify where your customers are browsing. If it's a physical space like a mall, then it's the directory kiosks and the physical layout of the mall itself. If your mall has a movie theater, for example, having your restaurant near or adjacent to that center of entertainment is smart marketing. As consumers come into the movies, they'll "discover" your restaurant nearby or adjacent to the theater and be more likely to stop by before or after the movie. This is why, for example, we see hotels next to Disneyland and fast-food restaurants next to High Schools. Adjacency increases the likelihood of a sale. If you're marketing in the digital space, then your to-do is to find the digital equivalent of physical adjacency. Popular blogs in your industry can be identified via Google searches that include the word "blog" as in "organic food blogs," or in the case of Jason's Cat Boarding Emporium, "cat blogs." Google even has techniques in its Display Network to pre-view keywords and search for blogs where your ads can appear.

Second, once you've identified the targets for your browse marketing, there are really two ways to get your content up in, or adjacent to, the relevant materials. You can *advertise*, using the Google Display Network (the largest advertising network on the Internet) via Google Ads (**https://ads.google.com/**). Or, you can create *content* and push it up into these blogs or other networks. The operative word here is "guest posting;" you are networking with the blog editors or owners to convince them to allow you to place an article on their blog for free. Tools like GuestPost.com can help you identify blogs that will accept contributed posts on topics that matter to you and your customers.

Podcasts are yet another media opportunity. Getting your CEO interviewed on relevant podcasts puts her message into the media stream; podcast listeners are browsing for new and interesting content and "just happen" to hear an interview by your CEO. The book interviews that fill late-night TV and radio shows like Terry Gross' *Fresh Air* on NPR are examples of browse marketing.

In summary, either you're paying for ads or you're using public relations tactics to get into media for free.

But it's not just textual blogs; it's also videos and social media networks. Another technique is what is called "**remarketing**." You can read about Google remarketing at **http://jmlinks.com/41z**. Remarketing also exists on Facebook, using what is called the "Facebook Pixel" (**http://jmlinks.com/42y**). (We discuss remarketing in detail in Chapter 19). In both cases, you're getting your marketing message out by surreptitiously "tagging" them via Internet cookies and then "following them" around the Internet as they browse for stuff. Remarketing is an advertising technique that is 100% browse. So your to-dos here would be to investigate remarketing and set up the infrastructure (the Google and Facebook cookie technology) that will allow you to remarket.

The third to-do is the message itself. The customer isn't proactively searching for your product or service! They're browsing, looking at things adjacent to your message. So your message must begin with a textual or visual "hook" that is compelling enough to grab their attention. Grabbing their attention is the hardest part of the message. Next, once you've gained their attention, you need to get them to leave what they were doing and click over to your blog, video, image, etc., and become engrossed in your full marketing message. In constructing your ads, a compelling "hook" gets the reader or viewer to begin the journey away from the content they were consuming and towards the marketing message you want to offer. For non-advertising content, it's a soft sell environment. Hearing an interview with your CEO on a podcast should be compelling enough to get that listener to Google your company and begin an inquiry. So, what's your hook? Where's your browse?

MEASURE: What They Browse, What They Like, What They Do

Measuring with respect to browse involves these same three aspects. You want to continually measure, for example, whether the sites or venues you are putting your efforts into are truly where your customers are browsing. If it's blogs, are you on the right blogs? If it's YouTube channels, are you on the right YouTube channels? If it's something in the real world, like a billboard on Highway A vs. Highway B, is your billboard on the right Highway? Or if it's in the mall, are you adjacent to the right stores, or if it's on Amazon, are you being featured as a "people also bought" vis-a-vis the right competitive products? Measure whether you're in the right places, and be on the lookout for new opportunities.

Second, are you using the right method to acquire visibility? Does straight advertising work better than organic or native placement? People often talk about using influencers or product placement, for example, but this soft-sell might not work as well as a hard sell through simple ads. The return on investment needs to take into account every aspect from target identification, to content production, to placement. Ads are expensive out of pocket, but organic efforts such as influencer marketing involve sweat equity, and this can be even more expensive than mere dollars. Does paid or organic yield a higher return on investment?

Finally, is any of this generating increased brand awareness or even actual sales? Advertising on browse networks like Facebook, LinkedIn, Instagram, or Google's Display Network can be easily measured in their native analytics platforms as well as Google Analytics (as people hit your website), but even organic efforts such as guest blogging or podcast interviews should generate a measurable boost to brand awareness, sales inquiries, or actual sales. Browse isn't just "busy work" after all, but part of your integrated marketing effort to build your brand and sell more stuff.

Chapter 13
Twaggle: Build Your Marketing Plan

Hunters and fishermen pay a lot of attention to nature. Not just to their "targets," but to what their targets eat, where they live, what they're doing, and where they hide. As marketers, hopefully, we don't take this metaphor too literally. We're not hunters or even fishermen; we're persuasion engineers seeking to get our marketing message out there, where our customers are, and persuade them to begin a journey from awareness to interest, interest to desire, and desire to action (*AIDA* as it is known in marketing parlance).

The **twaggle**, therefore, of discovery is to continually *discover* your discovery paths. Your goal is to become a better hunter, a better fisherman or woman, and a better marketer by toggling between the theory and practice of discovery.

Think: Know Your Discovery Paths

Remember, there are five, and only five, discovery paths. Which ones do you initially think are relevant to your product or service? And which ones retain that relevance over time?

Trust. Are they sensitive to online reviews or other trust indicators? What are they, and how can you influence them in a positive direction?

Search. Are they searching for your product or service? Where and how?

Share. Do they share with friends or family their "love" of your product or service? How can you get them to do so? Are they sensitive to influencers, and, if so, to which ones?

Interrupt. Is what you have to offer not something that they search for, or something so new that they don't know to even search for it? Use interrupt judiciously as it can come across as rude, but don't avoid it as it can work.

Browse. Are they out there "browsing" content, such as reading blogs or watching YouTube videos, or having fun on Facebook? Or browsing in the real world, as in a shopping mall or along an interstate highway? Get your marketing message adjacent to what interests them and hook them with a persuasive headline or graphic.

Do: Implement the Details of Discovery

Search isn't simple, and neither is interrupt, browse, or any of the other paths. The "do" component of your twaggle is to drill down into all the details. If it's search, then you have to either learn search engine optimization or how to use Google Ads effectively. If it's search on Amazon, you have to learn how to optimize a product on Amazon or how to use the Amazon ad platform. The same would go for Yelp or an industry-specific directory like Findlaw. If it's interrupt, then you have to master the art and science of effective TV or YouTube ads in an age of distraction and millisecond attention spans, and so on and so forth. The "do" component is that the "devil is in the details" for each discovery path, and an abstraction such as "trust indicators" becomes a concrete action item such as how to encourage more Yelp reviews without running afoul of the Yelp terms of service, or how to write better ad headlines on Google Ads, or how to implement the Facebook pixel and remarket via Facebook.

Your to-dos are:

Revisit each of the five discovery paths. Identify which ones are where your customers are "hanging out." Within a given path, drill-down and be even more specific. If it's search, for instance, is it Google, Bing, Amazon, Yelp, or Avvo? If it's browse, which blogs? If it's influencers, which influencers? Craft a marketing message that works within the given discovery path and medium. Figure out the details of getting your message in the right place at the right time, either through advertising or through organic means such as public relations or SEO. Measure which broad discovery path is working best, and within each path, which venue works the best as well. Distinguish among the path, the medium, and the message as you can fail at any level.

MEASURE: Optimize Your Discovery Paths

The "measure" aspect of discovery paths has two components. First, be continually aware of new opportunities along each path. Should Google introduce a new advertising format, such as when they created "remarketing" a few years back, suddenly there's a new opportunity on a path such as browse. New paths will not emerge, conceptually, as there are only five conceptual paths; there really is nothing new under the sun. But new *subpaths* may emerge in the real world, as for example, when new digital marketing venues emerge (e.g., TikTok or Snapchat) or even changes in oldies but goodies such as personalized direct mail technology and print on demand.

Second, along each path, continually measure and optimize your efforts. Within the search path, it's pretty obvious that Google Ads (formerly called AdWords) constantly evolves and that you have to make an effort to read the latest books on Google Ads, take the latest webinars, and pay attention to the latest training on how to use the latest and greatest version of Google Ads. Ditto with advertising on Facebook, Twitter, and YouTube, or with more traditional forms of advertising such as print, TV, or trade shows. Keep informed on the paths that matter to you in a "big picture" sort of way. Free organic reach such as SEO or review marketing on Yelp also evolves and changes.

But also measure in a very detailed way by using tools such as call tracking and Google Analytics to discover what's working and what's not. What's generating better brand awareness? What's generating sales or sales leads? Measure what you're doing that's working on a path, and learn how to do it better. And if it doesn't work, like a good hunter or fisherman, throw it back in the water and try again. Learning what doesn't work is as important a skill as measuring and learning what does.

SECTION III
DEPLOYMENT

This has been a book not only about better thinking about how to market your business, but better doing and better measuring. Accordingly, in Section III, we survey the media opportunities that exist for today's marketer. All Chapters in this Section are but the briefest of introductions to each topic yet have pointers to more detailed information online. For example, we investigate the basics of Search Engine Optimization or "SEO" with pointers to the official Google *SEO Starter Guide*, and we explain how Personal Selling is alive and flourishing in both digital and non digital formats. Throughout, we're learning to "fish" for customers and to "fish where the fish are."

Chapter 14
Content

I n his 1964 classic, *Understanding Media*, Marshall McLuhan argued that "the medium is the message." I can't do justice to McLuhan's incredible book, but suffice it to say that each medium – e.g., TV, print, radio, a conversation, even a light bulb – has a profound effect on how content can be communicated and understood. Video, for example, is excellent at conveying emotion. Photos are great for fun, impactful information but not great at complex or detailed information. The written word is great at details but not as easy to grasp as a photo or video. What you are trying to communicate is constrained by the media "container" it has to fit into.

In this Chapter, we'll examine content types such as images, blog posts, website pages, menus, signage, etc., against the marketing goals of building your brand and selling more stuff. As you look at media abstractly (devoid of content), you will begin to see how the "medium is the message," that is, how the *medium* itself (images, blog posts, website pages, menus, signage, etc.) influences how you can best structure your *message*.

THINK: Content and its Attributes (in No Particular Order)

You may not consciously be aware of it, but the medium into which you "pour" your content affects the content itself. Creating a video, for example, is quite different from creating a blog post. Creating a billboard is quite different from writing your restaurant menu. Drafting a tweet is very different from writing a long-form "frequently asked questions" document for your website. And constructing your booth at the annual trade show is very different from figuring out the telemarketing scripts your sales staff will use in personal selling.

As you create content, become aware of how the "medium" influences the "message." Don't commit the error of trying to force a message into a medium that is not hospitable.

Let's review some key types of content and investigate how the "medium" influences the "message" throughout the "content marketing" process.

Website Content. In the digital age, it should come as no surprise that your website is foundational to your content marketing strategy. Even a brick-and-mortar pizza restaurant or a cat boarding emporium, for example, will rely on its website for conversions. Generally speaking, the website is the "landing page" that receives traffic generated by other marketing efforts such as SEO, social media posts, advertising, and even word of mouth. Its primary purpose is to persuade customers to the next step – usually a sale or a sales lead. Finally, to look at your website, in terms of content, it's not one pure type of content but rather an amalgam of text, images, and often video.

Landing Pages. Again, either for conversions, for SEO, or for social media, you want to look at your website and optimize the content of your landing pages. Someone does a search on Google for "San Francisco Cat Boarding" and then clicks over to your landing page. Does it successfully persuade them to take the next step of setting up an onsite tour or booking an appointment? Why or why not? Each landing page on your website should be a persuasive symphony of the printed word, images (photographs), and/or video.

Blog Posts or Articles. Here, again, you have content that lives on the website and can combine text, images, and/or video. But blog content can either be optimized for SEO and conversion or optimized for social media and sharing. A blog headline can either be "search" heavy (containing the target keyword) or "share" heavy (containing emotional hooks or levers to spur interest and sharing).

White Papers / Case Studies / Customer Success Stories. Especially if your business is more professional, B2B, or just more "intellectual," you can create content such as in-depth white papers that explain industry issues and showcase your product or service as a solution. Even better, you can use a "tip of the iceberg" strategy with just a teaser headline and summary visible without registration and then force registration before the user gets access (and you get her email). If a customer is ready to read a white paper or case study, then he is in rational mode and looking for an analytic statement of why your product solves a need or addresses a desire. This medium heavily favors rational content.

eBooks. Semantically similar to white papers, the advantage of eBooks is that they can "live" on your website or on Amazon, and can either be a path to revenue directly (e.g., you make money by selling the eBook), or can be used as "gated content" to capture email addresses and sales leads. And an eBook can discuss something not as "intellectual" as a white paper, such as an eBook on how to create the best family holiday ever, how to choose the best dog, or even whether a hair transplant might work for you.

Brochures or Datasheets. Many companies still produce print brochures or datasheets, and these can live either online or in print (or both). In most cases, they will rely more on logic than illogic, often showcasing product features and benefits. As they are far down the sales funnel and closer to a sale, they tend to favor the "left" logical brain over the "right" creative brain function.

Signage. Don't forget the real world if you are a brick-and-mortar store. Signage matters. The billboard on the road, the signage in front of your store, your employee uniforms, even the cleanliness of your windows – all this "signage" has the persuasive purpose of being a "trust indicator" and convincing a person to stop in or be in the mood to buy. Take the example of a billboard. The "medium" influences the message – it has to be very short, very visual, and evocative. In the blink of an eye, it has to communicate a message. The message cannot, therefore, be very complicated.

Menus. If you're a restaurant, your menu can live online, on the digital signage if you're fast food or casual dining, or on the printed menu that a customer holds in his hand. The menu has the rational constraint of explaining the available food options. But it is also an opportunity for trust indicators and an opportunity to "upsell" customers on desserts or drinks.

Webinars, eCourses, Real-World Seminars, Podcasts. Free or even paid online learning is quite a trend, and many companies promote and host webinars that address common desires and pain points, answer questions, and showcase a product or service. Whether this training occurs in a short webinar, a more lengthy eCourse or a real-world seminar will impact the nature of the content provided; even more so, you need to decide whether it is a "pre" or "post" sale event, and to the extent that it occurs before the sale, it needs to persuade potential customers to take the next step of either a one-on-one consultation or purchase. Because webinars combine the spoken word with visual props such as PowerPoint slides, they can mix emotional and rational content plus begin to build a "personal relationship" with potential buyers.

Personal Selling. Your employees will often interact with customers directly, face to face or if not face to face, at least over the phone and email. Here the medium provides the opportunity to build a personal relationship; people like to buy "from their friends," and this medium provides the opportunity to nurture friendships (whether real or not).

FAQs or Long-Form Content. Similar to webinars but focusing on the printed word, FAQ (frequently asked questions) documentation or so-called "long-form content" is a beefy type of content that is very SEO and social media-friendly. If you or your company is an expert in a given domain, and customers commonly have identifiable questions, consider creating long-form content. Note that, in most cases, this media choice will favor utility and logic over emotion and illogic.

Email / Email Newsletters. Emails are the most intimate of digital communication, as people are leery of "spam" or "unsolicited email." Note the structure of an email starting with the sender and subject line (*its job: to get attention and get it opened*), then the persuasive content in the body (*its job: to get the customer to the next action*). Email can either be automated or a one-on-one effort. *Email newsletters*, as opposed to single emails, are a type of email sent, usually to your superfans or more motivated customers. The big constraint of email is getting it to the sender in the first place and getting the sender to open it at all.

Infographics / Instructographics. If you don't know what an *infographic* is, simply go to Google and type in your *keyword* plus *infographic* as in "organic food infographic." Infographics are visual charts or data displays that focus on explanatory content; *instructographics* are a type of infographic that explains "how to" do something, as in "instructographic how to tie a Windsor knot." Because they are fun and useful, they tend to be highly shared on social media. Their nature makes them focus on "how to" content and/or analytic content that relies on text and graphics.

Ads on Google. Ads on Google, Bing, or Yahoo, consist of a headline, two lines of text, a visible URL, and a few additional site links or call out text elements. You might not think of ads as part of your content marketing, but ads are an essential element. Their job? First, to get attention and, second, to get the click to your website. Evaluate your ads as to whether they are achieving these two purposes. The medium constrains the message: the very short thirty or so characters in a Google ad headline give you little room for complex ideas.

Ads on Social Media. Ads on Facebook, Twitter, LinkedIn, Pinterest, or Instagram usually combine a visual element like a photo or video plus a couple of lines of text. In this way, the "medium" allows for a combination of visuals plus text and your marketing message has the goal of increasing brand awareness, getting a click to your social media Page or website, or both. Because they are on social media and because they can contain images and/or videos, they can be more "emotional" than ads that appear in text-only format on Google, Bing, or Yahoo.

Curated Content. Positioning oneself as a "helpful expert" is a common branding goal of both key personnel and your company. Curated content can exist, for example, as a blog post of the "top ten" resources for such-and-such, a YouTube unboxing video, or even the systematic sharing of other people's content on social media like Facebook or Twitter. Your content production is constrained by identifying and summarizing the content of others, plus (if possible) adding a twist that promotes your own brand. This medium orients itself towards all content that positions you as a "helpful expert."

Demos, Instructional Videos, or How-Tos. Because customers often want to try before they buy, you can create instructional materials (in print or video format) that walk them through step-by-step. A manufacturer of lawnmowers, for example, can showcase the latest lawnmower features (and benefits). Note that this content can be a live demo in a real store, a video on YouTube, or even an infographic. And note that these types of videos can be either "before" or "after" the sale. If "before," then their purpose is to "show" (not "tell") how useful your product or service is and motivate a potential customer to take the next step of becoming a "sales lead" or making an actual purchase.

Datasheets or Product Brochures. Similar to an instructional video, a datasheet is a printed listing of features and benefits, usually with a product summary. This is very "left brain" as a medium, so your content should emphasize a systematic, logical explanation of features and benefits.

Quizzes or Personality Tests. Popular on social media (especially Facebook), quizzes or personality tests allow you to engage your audience in questions and answers. A quiz can be more "left brain" by emphasizing features and benefits vis-à-vis customer desires or needs, or more "right-brain" by emphasizing something fun or creative. In any case, the persuasive goal is to gain attention, build engagement, and lead the customers towards more awareness or desire for your product or service.

Giveaways, Discounts, or Special Offers. Everyone loves a good deal. This is why car companies bombard us with "special offers" around each and every holiday throughout the year, and why department stores like Macy's insist (perhaps disingenuously) that each and every sale is the "biggest sale of the year." Offering a giveaway such as a BOGO (buy one, get one free), a discount, or a special offer adds urgency to the marketing message and attempts to provoke an action such as a purchase or an in-store visit. Plus, on social media, giveaways and special offers can encourage sharing among customers as one customer seeks to "help out" his or her family, friends, or business colleagues. The medium, however, constrains the message. It has to be short and to the point: what does the customer get?

PSAs (Public Service Announcements). We live in an era of "corporate citizenship." Brands seek to portray themselves as "good corporate citizens" (with an implicit message that you can support this or that cause by patronizing this or that business). This is why big brands endorse popular causes such as gay rights or environmentalism, seeking to attach their brands via a "halo effect" to current social trends. PSAs that are "sponsored" by brands are an example of such content and can live on YouTube as video ads or be as simple as logos affixed to the web pages of non-profits. The goal? Build the brand identity by attaching it to a social good.

Live Streams. Facebook, YouTube, LinkedIn, and Twitter all now offer live stream capabilities. This is generally done via video, but in the case of Twitter can be a so-called "Twitter chat." The "live" element lends a sense of urgency to the content and creates the feeling that participants are special. Live streams are, therefore, a great way to nurture superfans who may share your brand message with others. The constraint is that because it's live, the user has to also be available at the same moment in time that you are.

Photos. A picture, as they say, is worth a thousand words. Many of the social networks have gone visual, with nearly all posts containing a photo or image. In this way, the medium emphasizes visual communication over the written word. But even in the "real world," photos are useful. Witness the common practice among pizza restaurants in New York of having photos of famous people ("influencers") on their walls as trust indicators. Because they are images and not text, photos tend to be better at conveying simple emotional content and not complex textual content.

Social Media Posts. A post on Facebook, Twitter, or LinkedIn usually consists of a headline, a few lines of text, a photo or video, and a link to a website URL or blog post. In this way, you are writing the "headline" for additional content, and so the purpose of your social content is to grab attention and move the customer to the next stage of the sales funnel. Become a better headline writer as in "man bites dog," not "dog bites man" (i.e., unusual or counterintuitive headlines pack more punch). Social media favors emotion, with the possible exception of LinkedIn, which favors factual reason given its B2B nature.

Memes. Memes are Internet posts that usually contain a stereotypical or easily recognized person or graphic, plus a few lines of text. They are usually humorous and leverage counterintuitive logic to spur sharing. To browse meme ideas, simply Google "meme" plus a few of your keyword themes. Brands can use memes to leverage humor as a catalyst for social sharing. A meme can't be complex. A meme must be simple and emotional.

Presentations. A presentation is usually a walk-through of product benefits and features, or it can be a corporate take on a timely topic in your industry. Think industry **trade show presentations**, but these can be transferred into online formats on YouTube, Slideshare, or even into a blog post. **Webinars** are yet another form of presentation. In this way, presentations are not necessarily a way to attract attention but rather to persuade customers once you have their attention. So think of your presentations as having to work in combination with some other strategy (e.g., email, advertising, social media posts) to attract attendees, first, and persuade them, second.

Customer Banter. The interaction between your sales staff and the customers is a form of content! When a salesperson walks up and says, "Can I help you? Are you looking for anything in particular?" – that's a form of content, or when at the checkout, he says, "You should follow us on Twitter for coupons and special deals. Here's how." Pre-think the customer-to-salesperson banter and leverage it for your persuasive goals, whether that is to upsell to another product or service or to use that real-world interaction to garner a review on Google or Yelp or a follower of your Twitter or Facebook page. Conversation is persuasion, too.

Telemarketing or Cold Calls. This is a form of interrupt media. Your sales staff pre-identifies target prospects and then calls them "cold." The persuasive task is first to gain their attention (i.e., get them to listen and not hang up the phone), and then to move them down the sales funnel. Telemarketing can be completely cold, or it can be follow-up calls from feedback forms on a website. Like so much content, don't think of telemarketing in isolation. Think of it as a team sport; how can your website feedback forms support better cold calls, making it easier for your sales staff to start the conversation and make the sale? And what type of scripts will work best, from the "icebreaker" first words to subsequent persuasion? Telemarketing, like email, is constrained by the difficulty of the first few seconds aimed at getting the recipient not to disengage.

Quotes. Especially on Facebook, LinkedIn, and Instagram, there is now a cottage industry of quotations placed over images. This type of curated content positions your brand as "in the know" and a "helpful expert." Quotes by famous people or industry experts are an easy and often overlooked form of content. Foundr magazine on Instagram (**https://www.instagram.com/foundr/**) has built nearly its entire social following on this strategy.

Press Releases. Using paid syndication services like NewsWire or EIN, you can create formalized press releases and send them out to interested bloggers and journalists. The goal of this type of content is to raise awareness in the media, as well as influence the search engines for SEO. Press releases are a type of blog post on steroids.

Apps. There's an app for that. Yours. Big brands from Yelp to McDonald's to Chick-fil-A have created their own proprietary apps for better customer engagement. They are useful to stay top of mind with customers, especially SuperFans. Creating an app is easier than ever, but the content question is why will customers want your app, and what will they do with it once they have it? An app helps you stay top of mind with your best customers and then communicate with them not only to bring them back to your brand but also, perhaps, to share content with their friends. **Snapchat** and **Instagram stories** also have this function.

Contests & Challenges. Contests and challenges are a big way to generate buzz on social media, especially Instagram, Twitter, TikTok, and Facebook. By creating a contest or a challenge and giving away something of value (it might be just free publicity for your best customers), you encourage social sharing. The persuasive purpose of contests is thus promotion, so think of connecting contests to a next step such as signing up for your email newsletter, following you on Instagram or Facebook, or subscribing to special offers by text.

Testimonials and Customer Reviews. Testimonials and customer reviews are trust indicators. Once you have good ones, showcase them on your website. Or, you'll notice in the real world how restaurants such as the Five Guys burger chain reprint positive reviews and display them for customers to read throughout the restaurant. Online, many companies have a "testimonials" tab to showcase positive customer stories. But understand that reviews on third-party sites like Yelp, Glassdoor, or Airbnb are perceived as more accurate and believable than those on your own website. Where a review lives, in short, impacts its credibility.

Video. Like photos, video is a medium unto itself. Separate the content from the location. Video can "live" on YouTube, on Facebook, on LinkedIn in a "native" format. And if a picture is worth a thousand words, a video is worth ten thousand. Video excels at content that is easier to "show" than to "tell," and content that has a heavy emotional flavor. Videos are among the most highly shared forms of content, and because people share what touches their emotions, viral videos are heavily about emotional content.

Podcasts. One of the more significant trends of recent years is the explosion of audio content, both as audiobooks on Audible and as podcasts. You can either create your own podcast for your own customers or try to book yourself as a guest on the podcasts of others. In any event, because podcasts and audiobooks are 100% aural, you need to conceptualize the conversational aspects of your message – what can be discussed or talked about with words in oral form vs. what might be better shown in a picture or video.

Content is all around you. The form it takes influences the message it can convey. Look around you at the real world, at interactions between customers and employees, at social media, at search engines, at video, at images, at textual content, at trade shows, at radio, etc., and inventory the "content opportunities" that can help your brand. Which works best for your company? What are the requirements and parameters of each? How can you fit your *message* to the *medium*?

The Four Types of Content

There's another way to look at content. As opposed to looking at the content type itself, you can categorize content by who owns it. First, there is **your own content**. This is content that you, yourself, fully own and produce such as when you write a blog post, you create a photograph, or you shoot a video. The advantage of "your own content" is that you create it and you can "spin" the marketing message to your advantage. The disadvantage is that it can be expensive and/or time-consuming to produce.

Second, there is **other people's content**. This is a curated content strategy in which you use tools such as Feedly, Google News, or Buzzsumo to curate the not-so-good content from the really good content, and share only the good stuff with your followers usually through social media such as LinkedIn, Facebook, or Twitter.

Third, there is **UGC** or **User Generated Content**. This is content you encourage your customers, fans, and superfans to create around your brand. A good example of this is how REI uses the hashtag *#optoutside* on Instagram to encourage customers to share photos of themselves out enjoying the outdoors (and implicitly promote the REI brand). Contests and challenges are another common example of UGC. The advantages of UGC are that your customers are creating it so it's relatively inexpensive and people tend to believe what their friends, family, and business colleagues say (over what brands say). The disadvantages are that it can be hard to get going and you don't fully control it, so there is a danger here that UGC might not promote your brand in a positive way.

Finally, there is **interactive content**. This is when, on social media, your brand or your employees "interact" with customers by liking, commenting on, or sharing the posts of customers. It's also the conversations your employees have with customers in the store. It's conversational in nature, yet behind the scenes, an effort can be made to persuade customers to make purchases.

DO: Create a Content Marketing Plan

Content might seem overwhelming once you realize just how many options you have. Your **to-dos** are to first, work at a high level of generality, and second, to work at the level of individual pieces of content. First, looking at your content choices, keep in mind the four big categories of your own content, other people's content, UGC, and interactive content, and identify your best opportunities. What can you produce cheaply? What type of content is most likely to achieve your marketing objectives? And how do different pieces of content such as email blasts and videos work together along the sales funnel?

Your content marketing plan should outline the content you need to produce, who will produce it, where and when they will produce it, and its role in the persuasive process. Second, drill down into individual pieces of content (photos, blog posts, videos, signage, even scripts to assist telemarketers or sales staff), and organize each piece of content. What will the blog post headline be? What is its purpose? What will the textual elements of it say? Will it have embedded photos or videos? As you begin to produce content for your marketing efforts, think "content production factory," not "individual artist."

The twaggle when it comes to content is to keep both the "big picture" elements in mind as, at the same time, you produce the nitty-gritty of content across media. Throughout, be cognizant of how the "medium is the message." Video content needs to favor visuals and emotions. The written word can convey complex, rational ideas. Photos have to be instantly understandable, and so on and so forth.

MEASURE: The ROI of Content

Content produced for marketing is content with a purpose. You're not an artist producing art for art's sake. You're a marketer producing content for the sake of marketing. Which content are you producing that's cheap? Which content is expensive or hard to make? Is that content producing the desired effect? If so, how? If not, why not? Take a particular piece of content, such as a video you produce for YouTube. Is it getting viewed? Is it encouraging interaction such as thumbs up / thumbs down, comments, or shares? Why or why not? Is it encouraging people to move down the sale funnel towards the next action, such as a click from YouTube to your Website?

Is it easier to make a video for YouTube or a series of photos for Instagram? Is it easier to produce a digital menu for your restaurant or a special coupon offer for the website? You have a range of content choices and a range of messages you can embed in that content. Compare the ease of use with the effectiveness of the content to get at your ROI (return on investment).

Take an email that you send out to your email list, for instance. Is it opened? If it's opened, is it read? If it's read, is the next action taken? The "measure" component of content marketing is to analyze your total content marketing strategy as well as individual pieces of content and determine the ROI or return on investment. You can (and should) analyze each piece of content you produce against the return on investment (does it build your brand? does it promote you? Does it lead to a sales lead or sales inquiry?). Content is expensive to produce, not just in terms of money but in terms of blood, sweat, and tears (effort). Evaluate what works (and produce more of it) and what doesn't (and produce less, or none, of it). Evaluate your media choices, your messages, the fit, and what gives you the biggest bang for your buck

Chapter 15
The Twaggle of Content

You can't do marketing without content, and you can't (*or at least shouldn't*) do content without goals. The **twaggle** of content is to produce a lot of content systematically yet verify that it all works towards your ultimate marketing goals of building your brand and selling more stuff. Content for the marketer is not an "end in itself" but rather a "means to an end." Your content should "build your brand" to (ultimately) sell more stuff.

THINK: Learn the Logic of Content

Content is persuasion. It's that simple and that complicated.

Learn its rules and be systematic as a content producer. Grasp basics such as:

People can be rational, but they aren't always rational. Some – but not all – marketing content should speak to "Features and benefits" is the most common structure here. **People are "predictably irrational."** Master the logical fallacies. Deploy them as needed in your content marketing. Figure out your comfort level with the ethics of this fact. **The medium is the message.** A video is not a blog post, and a blog post is not a booth at a trade show. Pour your content into the medium and adjust it accordingly.

Use different content at different stages. Content at the early stages of the customer journey has different goals than content at the later stages. Similarly, content along each discovery path has a different rhythm. An ad on Google isn't the same as a telemarketing script to interrupt someone's lovely dinner. **Be systematically lazy.** Figure out what content your company can produce cheaply and systematically. Get the biggest bang for your content buck. Is it photos or blog posts? Is it User Generated Content or curated content? **Measure what works.** Measure what works, and do more of it. Revise or kill what doesn't work. Do not become emotionally invested in your content; you're a marketer, not an artist.

Nurture content types. Obviously, creating your own content should be a priority. Text, blog posts, photos, and videos are critical types of content you can produce yourself. But you should also work on curated content (identifying the content of others to position your brand as a "helpful expert), as well as interactive content (interacting with prospects and customers online). The Holy Grail, of course, is UGC (User-generated content). How can you encourage customers to write reviews on Google or Yelp, spontaneously post to Facebook or Instagram, snap selfies using your product or service, create videos about your brand on YouTube or TikTok and so on and so forth? Contests? Challenges? Branded hashtags? All of the above?

DO: Create a Content Marketing Machine

The "do" part of content is to think "content machine," not "lonely artist." The **twaggle** is to keep in mind the rules of content, on the one hand, and your specific persuasive objectives, on the other. This works both at the high level of generality (e.g., your content marketing plan) and the low level of generality (e.g., a specific piece of content like a tweet or a blog post). You need both a "grand vision" and a "specific task." In the age of SEO and social media, we all need a lot of content, and we need a Disney-like content marketing machine, not a Picasso-like artisan methodology to succeed.

Be lazy. Identify types of content you can create easily. Create a curation system so that you can feed content into your platform. Set aside a few hours each day or week to respond to user content online. And brainstorm contests, challenges, and branded hashtags that make it "easy" for influencers, superfans, and customers to talk about your brand online. **Don't go it alone.** Your "content marketing machine" is a team effort of you, other employees at the customer, influencers, superfans, customers, and even prospects.

MEASURE: Measure the ROI

Content doesn't exist just for its own sake. Evaluate whether your content is working at the high level of generality (is your content "strategy" working?) and at a specific level of content (is this individual video achieving the desired effect?). The **twaggle** is to simultaneously have a *content strategy*, produce *individual pieces of content*, and *evaluate* the ROI of every part of your content marketing process. Is your content marketing building your brand, leading customers down your sales funnel towards a sales inquiry or a sale? If so, do more of it. If not, tweak it until it does.

SURVEY OFFER

CLAIM YOUR $5 SURVEY REBATE! HERE'S HOW -

- Visit **http://jmlinks.com/survey**.
- Take a short, simple survey about the book.
- Claim your rebate.

WE WILL THEN -

- Rebate you the $5 via Amazon eGift.

~ $5 REBATE OFFER ~

~ LIMITED TO ONE PER CUSTOMER ~

SUBJECT TO CHANGE WITHOUT NOTICE

RESTRICTIONS APPLY

GOT QUESTIONS? CALL 800-298-4065

Chapter 16
Google Ads

Recall that the "**Search Path**" is when customers are pro-actively searching for a solution to their need or desire. The customer is going away to Cancun, and they need a place to stash the cat, so they search for "cat boarding" and hopefully discover *Jason's Cat Boarding Emporium*. Obviously, the primary method by which people *search* for information nowadays is **search engines**, and the primary *search engine* is Google. If search matters to you, then you need to work on getting your website to the top of search engines. **SEO** (*Search Engine Optimization*) and **Google Ads** (*advertising on Google*) are the two techniques that make this possible. Since advertising on Google is simpler and faster than SEO, let's look at Google Ads first.

THINK: Identify Your Keywords and Master Google Ads

Search in the digital world starts with **keywords**. Is it "cat boarding" or "cat hotels?" Is it "knee pain" or "knee doctor?" Is it "San Francisco," "SF," or just "near me?" Keywords matter for both search engine optimization and Google Ads, so you have to know your keyword targets in very specific detail. Here's some keyword theory for you:

An **"educational" keyword** is used at an early stage of the customer journey. A customer has a problem with his knee, for example, so he goes to Google and enters "knee pain." These are high-*volume* but low-*value* search keywords.

A **"transactional"** keyword is used close to a buy decision. The customer searches for "knee surgery" or even "best knee surgeon in San Francisco." He's close to buying something or at least close enough to be willing to listen to a sales presentation. These are *high-value* but *low-volume* search keywords.

A **"reputational"** or **"branded" keyword** may be used just before the buy decision. A customer searches Google for "Jason's Cat Boarding Emporium reviews" or just "Jason's Cat Boarding Emporium" (or "Doctor Alex Ventovich, Knee Surgeon in San Francisco"). These are when the customer is vetting the potential company, product, or service to determine if it's a good decision to buy.

Notice how the type of keyword used follows the customer journey from awareness to interest to desire to action. To be good at search, you must be good at keyword discovery and keyword organization. Visit the keyword section of my Dashboard at **http://jmlinks.com/dashadwords** for a list of free, fun tools for keyword discovery. Your first to-do is to identify your keywords, especially your transactional keywords, and to build a keyword list or "keyword worksheet."

Because Google is the market leader, we'll focus on **Google Ads,** formerly known as AdWords, Google's pay-per-click advertising product (though Yahoo / Bing have their own product). To set up a Google Ads account, visit **https://ads.google.com/**.

Conceptually, here's how Google Ads works. Users come to Google and type in **search queries** using **keywords**. Behind the scenes, **advertisers pre-identify target keywords** and write ads that are triggered by these keywords. Google **ranks the ads** to be displayed against a search query based on the bid per click (the amount each advertiser is willing to pay for the click from Google to their website) and the so-called "Quality Score," which is a function of the expected relevance of that ad as measured by the click-thru rate. The user **clicks on an ad** and goes from Google to the advertiser website. The **advertiser pays Google** 1¢ more than the bid of the advertiser beneath him (all things being equal).

It's much more complicated than this, but this is the basic outline. (To watch a short, official video on how Google Ads works, visit **http://jmlinks.com/42f**). Google Ads, as well as other types of search advertising as on Yelp, Amazon, and Bing/Yahoo, are all about identifying keywords that are relevant to your business, writing ads that attract customers, bidding enough to get your ads to show on relevant search queries, and getting clicks from search engines to your website.

There's a lot more to learn to use Google Ads effectively. See my *Google Ads Workbook* at **http://jmlinks.com/adwords** or access the official Google help files and tutorials at **http://jmlinks.com/42e**. Google also offers free online tutorials on Google Ads at **https://skillshop.withgoogle.com/**. Just take it with a grain of salt, as it is pretty salesy!

If you decide to advertise on Google, be wary of key "gotchas" that can cost you a lot of money:

Run only on the so-called **Google Search Network**, not the *Google Display Network* (which is a group of non-Google sites like blogs) or *Google Search Partners* (which is a group of 2nd tier search engines). This is so that your ads appear only on Google.com itself and not on various third-party websites. Know your **keywords**, and run only on high-value, **transactional keywords**. Generally speaking, do not run on *educational keywords*. That is, run on "knee surgeon," not "knee pain," or run on "cat boarding," not "cats."

Use **correct keyword match types**, that is, inputting *[knee pain]*, or *"knee pain"* into Google Ads as your keyword triggers. Do not just type in keywords with no plus sign, no bracket, or no quote or Google may run your ads on irrelevant search queries and generate expensive but irrelevant clicks. To learn more about match types, see **http://jmlinks.com/42z**. Don't confuse getting **clicks** *(which is how Google makes money)* with getting **conversions** *(which is how you make money)*. Optimize for conversions, not for clicks, i.e., for quality, not A *click* is just a visit from Google to your website, whereas a *conversion* is when a website visitor either buys your product or service immediately or at least becomes a "sales lead" by filling out a feedback form.

Finally, be aware that – generally speaking – the return on investment from SEO is many factors higher than the return on investment from Google Ads, so prioritize SEO over Google Ads. Google Ads has advantages such as it is very fast to deploy, you can geotarget Google Ads to just customers in a specific zip code, city, or state, and it is more effective on the mobile phone than on the desktop, but generally speaking, it is inferior to SEO in terms of results.

DO: Identify Keywords and Deploy Google Ads

As you can see, the twaggle of keywords and Google Ads is that you can't easily separate the learning from the doing, or the doing from the learning. Here are two basic **to-dos**:

Research and formulate a **keyword worksheet** identifying your high-value, transactional keywords. Set up **Google Ads campaigns > Groups > Ads** that leverage the correct "match types" to run on transactional keywords that are likely to end not just in clicks but in conversions.

Nearly every business today will benefit from a strategic investment in Google Ads. Learn the rules of how Google Ads work and become proficient, if not an expert. **Twaggle** back to your business value proposition, buyer personas, and brand identity to understand whether and how Google Ads fits into your larger marketing strategy, especially the "Search Path." Because Google Ads cost money, just realize that you have to self educate on the pros and cons of the platform before jumping in with oodles of dollars.

MEASURE: Use Google Analytics and Google Ads Tools To See What Works

One of the best attributes of SEO and Google Ads is that both are highly measurable. Google's free analytics software, *Google Analytics* (**https://analytics.google.com/**), allows you to measure the path from click to website landing to website behavior or even a conversion, defined as a sales inquiry or an e-commerce purchase. For Google Ads (as opposed to SEO), Google Analytics can tell you which keywords caused clicks and which clicks became sales or sales inquiries. You want to know, for example, if you target the keyword phrase "best cat boarding in San Francisco," whether your website ranks at the top of Google for that phrase and if so, in what position in the organic and/or so-called "Google pack" results that often appear for local searches.

Assuming you've identified high value, transactional keywords, your metrics are:

Does your ad **rank** or **show** on Google for your target keyword search queries? You want your ads to show most of the time and at the top positions. If you rank, are you **getting the click**? Rank isn't worth anything if there is no search volume, or if there is volume, but you aren't getting clicks. If you get the click, does the website visitor **bounce** or **convert** (i.e., purchase something or at least become a sales lead)?

Google Ads integrates with Google Analytics very well, and Analytics provides even more data for Google Ads than it does for organic traffic. You can measure whether your ads are running vs. your target keywords, the exact keyword search queries that get people to your website and whether those search queries result in bounces (i.e., the customer leaves your website immediately) or conversions (i.e., sales inquiries or sales). Similar data is available in Google Analytics for Bing/Yahoo advertising.

You can learn a lot about Google Analytics for free. For example, Google publishes a robust learning site called "Google Analytics Academy" at **http://jmlinks.com/42d**. The point of your metrics is to learn whether you're targeting the right keywords, whether you're ranking, whether you're getting clicks and whether those clicks are converting. There are details and drill-downs for each of these aspects, but they constitute the key metrics.

Chapter 17
SEO (Search Engine Optimization)

S EO is the other way of getting to the top of Google search. As in the Google Ads scenario, the customer is going away to Cancun, and they need a place to stash the cat, so they search for "cat boarding" and hopefully discover *Jason's Cat Boarding Emporium*. Obviously, the primary method by which people *search* for information nowadays is **search engines**, and the primary *search engine* is Google. If search matters to you, then you need to work on getting your website to the top of search engines. **SEO** (*Search Engine Optimization*).

THINK: Identify Your Keywords and Master SEO and Google Ads

As with Google Ads, SEO begins with keywords. Is it "cat boarding" or "cat hotels?" Is it "knee pain" or "knee doctor?" Is it "San Francisco," "SF," or just "near me?" Keywords matter for both search engine optimization and Google Ads, so you have to know your keyword targets in very specific detail. Highly focused keywords, including geographic phrases if applicable, can be the most lucrative. Let's revisit keyword theory but from the perspective of SEO and not Google Ads.

An **"educational" keyword** is used at an early stage of the customer journey. A customer has a problem with his knee, for example, so he goes to Google and enters "knee pain."

These are high-*volume* but low-*value* search keywords. These are hard to optimize for via SEO.

A **"transactional" keyword** is close to a buy decision. The customer searches for "knee surgery" or even "best knee surgeon in San Francisco." He's close to buying something or at least close enough to be willing to listen to a sales presentation. These are *high-value* but *low-volume* search keywords. These are relatively easy to SEO for, especially if they are geographic in nature, as in "best cat boarding in San Francisco."

A **"reputational"** or **"branded" keyword** may be used just before the buy decision. A customer searches Google for "Jason's Cat Boarding Emporium reviews" or just "Jason's Cat Boarding Emporium" (or "Doctor Alex Ventovich, Knee Surgeon in San Francisco"). These are when the customer is vetting the potential company, product, or service to determine if it's a good decision to buy. As these are critical to the last step before a purchase or a sales inquiry, you must optimize for your branded keywords!

Notice how the type of keyword used follows the customer journey from awareness to interest to desire to action. To be good at search, you must be good at keyword discovery and keyword organization. Visit the keyword section of my SEO Dashboard at **http://jmlinks.com/seodash** for a list of free, fun tools for keyword discovery. Your first to-do is to identify your keywords, especially your transactional keywords, and to build a keyword list or "keyword worksheet."

Next, now that you know your keywords, where do you put them? **"On Page" SEO** is where SEO influences how you build a website that "speaks Google."

Start by reading the "Google SEO Starter Guide" at **http://jmlinks.com/googleseo** to learn the basics of "On Page" SEO. Here are some key points:

> **HTML Tags**. Place your keywords in the most important HTML tags such as the TITLE, META DESCRIPTION, HEADER, IMAGE ALT, and ANCHOR tags. By interweaving keywords into the appropriate tags especially on your homepage, your website begins to "speak Google" and communicate clearly the keywords for which you wish to rank.

> **Visible Content**. Write textual content on each page that contains your target keyword phrases. Google looks for websites that regurgitate the search query! Don't underdo this, but don't overdo it, either. The latter, called "keyword stuffing," can incur a Google penalty.

> **Cross-link on Keywords**. Referred to as "link sculpting," cross-link key pages to each other around keyword themes. This communicates to Google the themes of the website and consequently the themes of your products or services against search engine queries.

> In addition, optimize your **home page** to have keywords in the TITLE and META DESCRIPTION tags as well as tags on the visible page and visible page

content. Google pays a lot of attention to whether target keywords exist in text format on the homepage, including city names for geographically relevant search queries. Start a **blog** on your website and start blogging on your keyword themes, as Google prioritizes fresh content.

With some basic "On Page" SEO optimization done, your next **to-do** is to turn to **"Off Page" SEO**. Google rewards websites that have external validations, almost as if ranking on Google were an "election" and things like **links** to your website, social authority like having good **reviews** on Google or many Twitter followers, and social mentions such as being frequently tweeted by others counted as "votes." "Off Page" SEO is the art and science of getting other websites to link to you, getting happy customers to write reviews of your business on Google and, to a lesser extent, on Yelp (if local search matters to you), and bolstering your social media presence, especially on Twitter. Links and reviews are by far the most important aspects. To learn more about SEO, see my *SEO Workbook* at **http://jmlinks.com/seo**.

DO: Identify SEO-friendly Keywords and Deploy Them into Your Website

As you can see, the twaggle of SEO is that you can't easily separate the learning from the doing or the doing from the learning. Here are your **to-dos**:

Research and formulate a **keyword worksheet** identifying your high-value, transactional keywords. Optimize your **"On Page" SEO** by building a Google-friendly Website. Optimize your **"Off Page" SEO** by securing links, Google reviews, social mentions, and social authority. If local matters to you, be sure to claim and optimize your Google My Business listing at **https://www.google.com/business**. Securing positive customer reviews is essential! Along the way, you have to be rather cynical about SEO, as what Google tells you in its official documents can be incomplete at best and misleading at worst.

Nearly every business today will benefit from SEO, and almost every business can benefit from a strategic investment in Google Ads. Learn the rules of each game and deploy your SEO and/or Google Ads content strategically. **Twaggle** back to your business value proposition, buyer personas, and brand identity to understand whether and how SEO and Google Ads fit into your larger marketing strategy, especially the "Search Path."

MEASURE: Use Google Analytics and Google Tools To See What Works

One of the best attributes of SEO and Google Ads is that both are highly measurable. Google's free analytics software, *Google Analytics* (**https://analytics.google.com/**), allows you to measure the path from click to website landing to website behavior or even a conversion, defined as a sales inquiry or an e-commerce purchase.

For SEO, one unfortunate gap is that Google Analytics does not allow you to measure your **rank** on Google against target search queries. You want to know, for example, if you target the keyword phrase "best cat boarding in San Francisco," whether your website ranks at the top of Google for that phrase and if so, in what position in the organic and/or so-called "Google pack" results that often appear for local searches. Free rank-checking tools are available on the "rank tools" section of my dashboard (**http://jmlinks.com/seodash**). A good paid tool is the Whitespark platform at **https://www.whitespark.ca**. A well-organized and SEO-friendly website can then be measured against whether it ranks for its target keywords or not, and then more effort can be put into either "On Page" or "Off Page" SEO (or both) to get it to rank. It's not easy, but it can be done with knowledge and hard work. Be sure to sign up for Google Search Console (**https://search.google.com/search-console**).

Assuming you've identified high value, transactional keywords, your metrics are:

Do you **rank** on Google for your target keyword search queries? You want to rank at least on Page One (the top ten results), the top three (the best), or in the local pack (if a search is a local query like "accountants" or "cat boarding"). If you rank, are you **getting the click**? Rank isn't worth anything if there is no search volume, or if there is volume, but you aren't getting clicks. If you get the click, does the website visitor **bounce** or **convert** (i.e., purchase something or at least become a sales lead)?

SEO integrates with Google Analytics very well, with the exception of keyword data. Unlike the situation on metrics for Google Ads, Google does NOT share keyword data for inbound SEO-related queries. After the click, however, Google Analytics provides a wealth of data on user behavior. You can learn a lot about Google Analytics for free. For example, Google publishes a robust learning site called "Google Analytics Academy" at **http://jmlinks.com/42d**. The point of your metrics is to learn whether you're targeting the right keywords, whether you're ranking, whether you're getting clicks and whether those clicks are converting. There are details and drill-downs for each of these aspects, but they constitute the key metrics.

Chapter 18
Social Media Marketing

No new marketing technique has received more hype than **social media**. It seems that everyone is "on" Facebook, Twitter, Snapchat, TikTok, LinkedIn, Instagram, YouTube, etc.... and that every "smart marketer" is already making zillions of dollars through social media marketing. It also might seem that only twenty-something hipsters, dressed in all-black with ear gauges and thousands of Snapchat followers, can market on social media. Fortunately, you don't have to fall for the hype, and you don't have to be under thirty to succeed at social media. Social media marketing is exciting and can be powerful if you have a conceptual framework. (Since I have an entire book on this topic, the *Social Media Marketing Workbook* at **http://jmlinks.com/smm**, this Chapter provides only a high-level overview).

THINK: It's a Party with a Purpose

Comparing social media marketing to the art and science of throwing a party is a useful conceptual framework. Social media is a *party*, and you – the marketer – are the *party thrower*.

Take, for instance, the example of throwing a wedding. First, there are the **invitations**. Who's on the guest list? Who do you want to attract to your wedding, and how will you persuade them to come? Invitations parallel the *promotion strategy* you'll need to market a product or service on social media. How will you get customers to "show up" to your

Facebook Page, Twitter feed, or LinkedIn employee profiles? It's propaganda that a Facebook Page or YouTube Channel promotes itself. It doesn't, just as a successful party doesn't promote itself.

Second, there's the party **theme**. Is it a light, outdoor wedding, or a serious Catholic or Jewish ceremony full of pomp and circumstance? There's no right or wrong theme, only themes that match your brand. Similarly, there's no right or wrong *theme* for your Facebook or LinkedIn Page for your business. It needs to match your brand identity, and your brand identity needs to be consistent, website to Facebook, Facebook to Twitter, Instagram to YouTube, etc.

Third, there's *content*, which parallels the **food and entertainment** at a party. On social media, you'll need a lot of content – blog posts, photos, videos, quotations, clever posts, etc., just as at a wedding you need a lot of great food, toasts to the bride and groom, music, an amazing cake, party favors, etc. A lack of food or entertainment means no party. A lack of fun or compelling content means no social media marketing. You need a lot of great content to succeed at social media marketing.

Notice, here, that there's a mix of *your own content, other people's content, user-generated content*, and *interactive content*. If you go for your own content, you make your own food for the wedding. The plus is that when the compliments come in, they go to your brand. You're the cook, and you're the genius. If you cater the wedding, however, the compliments go to the catering company and only, secondarily, to you as the smart wedding planner that chose them. So it is with social media. You have your own content (*the plus is that you control it and it builds your brand, the minus is that it's hard to make*), you have the content of others (*wherein you curate fun and/or useful content that positions you as a "helpful expert" to your followers*), you have UGC content (*which is content your users spontaneously make*), and you have interactive content (*which is the back-and-forth between you and your customers as well as among your customers online*) UGC content is when people spontaneously rise to give toasts at the wedding; UGC on social media is when happy customers spontaneously share to your brand hashtag on Twitter, Instagram, or Facebook, or post cool stuff to LinkedIn that compliments your brand. There's also interactive content, like the banter among guests, the toasts and audience response, or between the happy newlyweds and guests in the receiving line. (Revisit Chapter 19 for more on content marketing).

A Party with a Purpose. Finally, there's one big difference between parties in the real world and "parties" on social media. Most of the time, we don't have ulterior motives at our real-world parties. We just want people to come to the wedding, to get along, and to celebrate the bride and groom as they take their vows. There isn't an ulterior motive. With respect to our "social media parties," however, there *is* an ulterior motive. We marketers are engaging in social media marketing to build our brand and, ultimately, sell more stuff. Most commonly, we are engaging in social media marketing to spread our brand message directly as well as leverage superfans to get them to spread our message to their friends, family, and contacts. Social media marketing is more like corporate launch parties than like weddings in this sense — they are "parties with a purpose." So, you, as the marketing manager, need to keep a keen eye on the **goals** of your social media efforts. How does this fit into your larger marketing plan? Is social media helping you either at building your brand or selling more stuff?

Another way to use social media is to **advertise**. Here, you are less interested in building your social media brand and more interested in approaching social media as you might a blog, Google or search advertising, or other forms of online advertising. You're placing ads on Facebook or Instagram, LinkedIn or YouTube, not to build your social media presence but to "offload" from social media to your website, e-commerce store, or other objective such as getting sign-ups for a webinar, although you can also use advertising to build your social presence on a network as well. So you can either advertise on Facebook to push users to your e-commerce store, or you can advertise on Facebook to grow the "likes" of your Facebook Page. Ditto for YouTube, Instagram, LinkedIn, etc.

The beauty is that the big social networks, especially Facebook, LinkedIn, YouTube, and Twitter, have a wealth of demographic information. For instance, you can target men aged forty to fifty, who live in Northern California and love dogs, or you can target engineers who are interested in proteomics, or busy young professionals who have kids and live in Utah, and so on and so forth. You define the audience you want to reach, and you "pay" as an advertiser to "push" your message in front of an audience via "interrupt advertising" (See Chapter 16). Because advertising is how each platform makes money, they all provide a cornucopia of help files on how to advertise. Just Google "How to advertise on Facebook," for example, and you'll end up at **https://www.facebook.com/advertising**. Just Google "advertise" plus the name of any of the other social media platforms, and *surprise, surprise, surprise,* they all have helpful websites full of information.

Whether you are going after free organic reach or paid advertising, it's worthwhile to look at each platform and define its culture, strengths, and weaknesses, as well as ask yourself whether your customers hang out on it:

Facebook. The largest social media platform with over two billion users, Facebook is all about friends, family, photos, and fun. Its strength is in its massive reach; its weakness is in the fact that it is very oriented towards friends and fun and thus works best if you are B2C. Organic reach is very difficult on Facebook since it is so crowded, but its advertising opportunities are second to none for reaching consumers.

Instagram. Owned by Facebook, Instagram prioritizes user photos and also focuses on friends, family, and fun. It's stronger in pop culture, fashion, and everything that lends itself to photos. Strengths are in its reach and positive, photogenic culture. Weaknesses are that it is not widely used outside of B2C, plus it has technical limitations such as the inability to include links in posts.

Twitter. Twitter's strengths are its dominance of news and its role as the "goto" place where journalists turn to find breaking stories. It is also strong in pop culture, though that role is being challenged by Instagram. Its weaknesses are that it is extremely noisy and has brand challenges when it comes to fake news and cyberbullying. Twitter is also used to communicate deals, special insider incentives for superfans and is strong in the "food truck" and "lunchtime" industries.

It is used heavily at trade shows and thus has a stronger B2B reach than Instagram or Facebook.

LinkedIn. LinkedIn is THE network for professional services and B2B. Its strength is the focus on everything professional and business. It's also strong for job seekers and recruiters. Its weakness is that people who are not actively looking for a job do not use it as often as they might, though it is trying to grow into "continuing education." LinkedIn is the ultimate online rolodex and can be used by sales staff first to identify prospects and then contact these prospects via paid recruiter accounts.

YouTube. YouTube is the dominant video platform online, though it is increasingly challenged by Instagram and Facebook native video. YouTube is the #2 search engine, and many people search YouTube for "how to" information. Three possible uses of YouTube are *supportive* (using YouTube videos to support your other efforts as a form of content marketing), *SEO* (optimizing YouTube videos to appear at the top of search), and *share/viral* (optimizing YouTube videos to increase social shares up to and including viral marketing).

Pinterest. Pinterest is the social platform for shopping, women, and do-it-yourselfers. Users, including brands, can have "idea boards," wherein they curate content around a topic such as "wedding dresses" or "dog toys." If your brand is visual and lends itself to e-commerce, Pinterest is a must-do network.

Yelp / Google My Business / Review Marketing. Yelp is the #2 social network, after Google, when it comes to local consumer reviews. Users review restaurants, bars, coffee shops, plumbers, accountants, attorneys, and others in the home service space. See Chapter 14 on "review marketing" for more info.

Refer to my *Social Media Marketing Workbook* (**http://jmlinks.com/smm**) for a detailed explanation of how to market on each platform. Suffice it to say here that each platform can be assessed as to whether your customers are using it, where the organic or free opportunities are, the content marketing strategy that best fits its culture, and whether advertising might be cost-effective for your business. Don't be afraid to ignore some social media platforms. Not every platform fits every business, and you're better off doing just a couple well than doing all of them poorly.

DO: Audit, Deploy, Engage

Social media marketing excels at the Share Path and at the Browse Path. Social Media is a great way to reach people, not in search mode, but as they browse information on their friends, family, or interests. It's also the primary mechanism for digital sharing, as when a topic "goes viral" and suddenly "everyone is talking about it."

For your "parties with a purpose," you have three basic **to-dos**. First, **audit** each network to determine whether your customers are using it, and, if so, how you can best spread your brand message. What are your customers talking about, commenting, and sharing? How might your brand message fit into their conversations? Identify *competitors* who are already on a network, as well as *companies to emulate*. A solid audit means going through each network (Facebook,

Instagram, LinkedIn, Snapchat, etc.), and answering the marketing question of whether or not your customers are there, what content ideas competitors and others can give you, and assessing the potential return on investment from embracing that network.

Second, once you've identified a network that shows potential, it's time to **deploy**. Access tutorials and online learning materials to understand the technical challenges and opportunities available to you as a business on each platform. Deployment is all about creating the structural shell you'll need for your social media marketing content. Set up your Facebook Page (Twitter account, Instagram account, YouTube channel, etc.), following best practices for cover art, profile picture, and other unique features such as tabs on Facebook or the unsubscribed trailer on YouTube.

Third, launch your participation with plenty of **compelling content** and a systematic **promotion strategy**. There's no such thing as an effective Facebook Page with no content, nor can there be a YouTube channel with no videos. You'll need your own content, other people's content, and ideally, even user-generated content or UGC. Content marketing is a key part of success at social media, and alongside content, you need a promotion strategy. How will you get the word out about your Facebook Page, your YouTube channel, or your LinkedIn employee profiles? The best account set up in the world and the most incredible content mean nothing if there is no systematic promotion behind them. Advertising is one option, but other options are working with influencers or superfans to share content designed to be easy to share or even viral in nature.

Finally, remember that it's a "party with a purpose." Connect your YouTube videos to defined calls to action on your website; make it easy for people to go from your Instagram bio to your e-commerce store. Connect your white papers promoted through LinkedIn to registration forms to capture contact names, emails, and telephone numbers. Although social media marketing is most useful for branding, it can be used as a sales channel by adding links to e-commerce websites and/or feedback forms for more information.

MEASURE: the ROI of Social Media Marketing

Don't let anyone tell you that social media marketing has no goals or that the goals cannot be measured! Staying top of mind, encouraging social shares, and getting customers to talk about your brand are common goals. It's a soft sell environment as opposed to the hard sell environment of Google advertising or even personal selling. That said, social media marketing can be measured.

For example, for each platform, are you growing your Page likes? Are people engaging with your content as measured by likes, comments, and shares for individual posts? If you are producing content that people find attractive, you should see an upward trend in each of these metrics. If not, it's not working. For a specific piece of content, you can drill down and, again, look at the likes, comments, and shares. Which posts are getting the most interaction and why? Produce more of the content people like and less of the content they do not. Or, if an entire platform isn't working, then abandon it, and put your efforts towards those platforms that are working. You might think that Facebook will be #1 for you, but you might discover that Instagram or Twitter works better and produces a higher ROI.

Beyond awareness or branding goals, you can also measure whether social media efforts are leading folks down the sales funnel. Using Google Analytics, for example, you can track whether you are getting clicks from Facebook to your website or e-commerce store and whether those are converting to sign-ups or even sales. This is especially true if you advertise. Ads on Facebook, LinkedIn, Twitter, and YouTube are measurable both via their internal advertising metrics and externally to your website via Google Analytics

Chapter 19
Remarketing

Movie and SciFi buffs saw the future in the 2002 film, "Minority Report," when Tom Cruise, a.k.a., Captain Anderton, walked into a shopping mall and was "greeted" by interactive ads that knew his name, understood his tastes, and offered him everything from cars to beer by shouting out lines at him like, "You could use a Guinness right about now." Besides being hunted by the PreCrime division, Anderton was being "remarketed to." **Remarketing** is a new form of advertising in which someone who showed interest in, yet *did not buy,* your product or service can be "remarketed to" by pushing ads across search and social media.

Used well, remarketing can be a powerful addition to your marketing mix. Remarketing and its cousin, retargeting, are targeting methods that work well with the "browse" or "interrupt" discovery paths.

THINK: Understand Remarketing vs. Retargeting

Remarketing and its twin, **retargeting**, are easy to understand. In *remarketing,* someone "touches" your website but does not convert; that is, they don't buy your product or service and/or they don't fill out a sales lead form. Perhaps they did a Google search for "cat boarding in San Francisco" and then clicked over to the website but didn't send an inquiry. Or perhaps they arrived at the website from a Facebook or Twitter ad. They didn't convert, but they touched the website, and unbeknown to them a little piece of code, a "cookie" in HTML speak, was placed on their browser, so the marketer could follow them as they visited other sites on the Internet. (Cookies are being phased out, but rest assured, Google and Facebook are working hard at alternative methods that can still follow customers around the Internet).

Retargeting is a similar concept, but here, large third-party companies set up "honeypots" or networks that snoop into user behavior by extrapolating from the websites they visit and the content they engage with to infer their demographics. A retargeting network then sells this data, and you can retarget to defined groups such as men aged 40-50 who like motorcycles or people who are "in the market" for new cars or holiday cruises.

We'll focus more on remarketing, the more common and useful of the two concepts; just remember, however, that in the blogosphere, the two terms are used interchangeably if incorrectly. You'll read a lot of posts that conflate the two. Just remember conceptually that *remarketing* is something you do via your own website; *retargeting* is something you purchase from an ad network.

Not surprisingly, the two big remarketing networks are Google and Facebook. In each system, you, as the webmaster, install some code from Google or Facebook to your website which tracks visitor behavior. In the Google system, you install Google code either from Google Ads or from Google Analytics, and this code inserts the tracking "cookies" on web browsers as people hit your website. To learn more about Google remarketing, visit **http://jmlinks.com/42g**. In the Facebook system, you install the "Facebook pixel," which similarly allows user tracking by Facebook. To learn about the Facebook pixel, visit **http://jmlinks.com/42h**.

In both cases, here is how it works behind the scenes:

The user hits your website (from any source). A secret "cookie" (or other remarketing technology) is placed on his browser so that he can be tracked. You, as the marketer, pay Google and/or Facebook to re-show ads to him as he traverses the Internet, visiting other websites like YouTube, Gmail, Instagram, Facebook, blogs, etc. The user re-sees ads for your company, product, and/or service. The user, hopefully, clicks on your ads. You get a *second* opportunity to sell him on your product or service, hence the "re" in remarketing.

From the user's perspective, you can immediately see that there are privacy concerns. Neither Google nor Facebook provides advertisers with "identifiable" user data such as email or IP addresses, but nonetheless, most people do not understand tracking on the Internet. People can get pretty freaked out by being tracked, so some caution is in order lest your brand is perceived as creepy.

Both large Internet companies also engage in **retargeting**, the selling of user demographic data to advertisers. Other third-party networks such as AdRoll (**https://www.adroll.com/**) also sell retargeting services. The logic is the same; it's just that step #1 listed above is not that customers hit your website, but rather that they hit websites in a network and are sorted, tracked, and categorized. Retargeting is generally less effective than remarketing for the obvious reason that in the latter, the user already hit your website one time and is thus "more qualified" and "more likely" to become a customer. Remember that, unfortunately, the terms have become intermingled and confused across the Internet even though they are conceptually distinct. I use "remarketing" to mean the idea of re-reaching people who have already visited your own website and "retargeting" to mean purchasing demographic targets from an ad network. But others use the terms incoherently and incorrectly, including in the official documentation by both Google and Facebook.

Conceptually, what is the best way to use remarketing? **Remarketing works best for high-value items that have a long sales cycle.** Here's an example: a luxury cruise. If you and your family are considering taking a cruise vacation, you are intending to spend many thousands of dollars and invest your time in the vacation. This is not a decision that you undertake lightly or immediately, as compared with purchasing a new case for your iPhone or selecting a pizza restaurant for tonight's pizza delivery. The sales cycle is "long," and the product is "high value." You might begin your search in February with some Google searches and visits to various cruise websites, check out their Facebook pages and Instagram feeds, and ask friends and family for recommendations. You might not make your decision for several weeks. So you might "hit" the website of Carnival Cruises or Royal Caribbean and not "convert," meaning not purchase a cruise nor even fill out a feedback form showing interest.

By using remarketing, cruise vendors can identify you and then show and re-show you ads about their products as you surf the web. First, you hit Carnival.com, and suddenly you see ads for cruises on YouTube, on blogs, on CNN, on

NYTimes.com, and even in Gmail. You're being remarketed to. You're being reminded of your interest in purchasing a cruise. Remarketing is a kind of constant reminder from an advertiser about a purchase you might just want to make.

As a marketer, therefore, ask yourself if your product is high value and has a long sales cycle from awareness to action. *Cat boarding*, for example, might qualify, but *cat toys* would not. *Hair transplant surgery* would qualify, but *shampoo* would not, and so on and so forth. (Note: there are restrictions on remarketing certain medical products or services, so not everything can be remarketed due to privacy concerns). Assuming that you fit the parameters of high value and long sales cycle, then you should set up remarketing. Setting it up on Google Ads allows you to advertise to people across the Google Display Network and show both text and image ads to likely prospects. The beauty is that you are only showing ads to people who have already hit your website, thus obviating many of the problems on the Display Network in terms of low-quality sites and fraud. To learn more about the Google Display Network, visit **http://jmlinks.com/42j**. On Facebook, you are essentially doing the same thing via the Facebook Pixel; it's just that Facebook is so big it refuses to be part of Google's network (of course). Generally speaking, you want to run remarketing on both Google's and Facebook's networks simultaneously.

As for **retargeting**, both Google and Facebook resell demographic information for ad targeting and placement. Via Google, you advertise on the *Google Display Network* and can identify various demographic targets via attributes like age, gender, and device types, affinities, in-market audience (i.e., people who are "in the market" for a purchase like a cruise or a new car), keyword matching, and similar audiences. To learn more, visit **http://jmlinks.com/42k**. Just remember that retargeting is much, much less effective than remarketing, and the Google Display Network is plagued with poor match types and even fraud. I would not, generally, suggest using it without reading the Chapter in my *Google Ads Workbook* on the Google Display Network.

As for Facebook, retargeting there is also demographically based. It is referred to as "audience targeting," while remarketing is a "custom audience" you build based on your Facebook Pixel. To learn about Facebook targeting options, visit **http://jmlinks.com/42m**. On both networks, just keep clear in your mind the difference between "remarketing" (showing your ads to people who have already visited your website) and "retargeting" (showing your ads to people based on attributes inferred by the networks). And keep in mind that the terms might be referred to incorrectly, even by Google or Facebook!

DO: Deploy Remarketing and Consider Retargeting

Assuming that all or at least some of your products are high value and have a long decision cycle, then you should consider remarketing. Regardless, I would recommend that you implement the Google Analytics / Google Ads code as instructed by Google and install the Facebook Pixel. These work in the background even if you do not have remarketing "on," and because it takes some time to build an audience, you want to start the process as soon as possible. In addition, if you decide to go forward with remarketing, you can either do it in a simple fashion (remarket to EVERYONE who touches your website) or in a more sophisticated way (remarket by segment – for example, ONLY to people who do not convert, ONLY to people who click on high-value pages, etc.). This avoids the annoyance of remarketing over and over again to people who have "already" purchased your product. You can also set limits on how frequently people see your ads as well as a time limit such as only show ads to them for one day or one week. This is to avoid creeping out your potential customers. Check the Google and/or Facebook documentation to implement so-called "frequency capping" correctly.

Once you have built the audience, you need to create the ads either on Google or on Facebook. On Google, you create a Google Display Network campaign and select "Audiences" as the targeting method, using your remarketing audience as the target. In terms of ad design, you can create your own text ads, upload image ads, or use the Google responsive ad builder to have Google create ads from your own website. Learn more about how to set up Google remarketing at **http://jmlinks.com/42p**. In Facebook, you use the Facebook pixel to create a "custom audience" and then "boost" a post, advertise your Facebook Page, and/or advertise your website to this "custom audience" of remarketable website visitors. Learn more about Facebook Custom Audiences at **http://jmlinks.com/42n**.

In addition, should remarketing work well for you, you might consider setting up retargeting. Just remember that using a network like AdRoll means you are reaching people who did NOT visit your website. They are thus generally not as qualified, and the return on investment is usually lower than remarketing to people who visited your website (and expressed interest) in the first place.

MEASURE: Use Google Analytics, Google Ads, and Facebook to Measure

Because remarketing is an advertising product, you want to measure it in the way you'd typically measure any online advertising effort. First, are you reaching the right audience? Remarketing and retargeting are, after all, just mechanisms to target people. So are you targeting the right people? Can you refine them further into those most likely to buy and pay to advertise only to that group? Separating the wheat from the chaff, so to speak, means refining your remarketing audience on Facebook and/or Google to distinguish between tire-kickers and those likely to buy. Second, test various ads in text, image, and video format. Which ads convert better and why? Aim to build on those ad messages that work and delete those that do not. Finally, measure the return on investment. How much money (as well as blood, sweat, tears, and efforts) are you putting into your remarketing efforts vs. what you're getting out? Remarketing and retargeting, to a lesser extent, work great for some products and services and fail to work for others. A keen eye on the return on investment is the ultimate metric of an ad dollar well spent.

Chapter 20
Word of Mouth

Word of mouth is often described as the most important or most powerful marketing channel, yet it is also the most frustrating to marketers. Customers may trust the recommendations of friends, family, and business colleagues, but it's hard for marketers to "influence the influencers" or "share to the sharers." The best that can be done for word of mouth in the non-digital or so-called "real world" is to provide incredible customer service and an over-the-top experience in the hope that "spontaneous" word of mouth will follow. That rule still applies in the digital world, but social media has given rise to eWOM (*electronic word of mouth*) and so-called *influencer marketing*. These new digital opportunities should be part of any up-to-date marketing plan.

THINK: Identify Why They'll Share, Who Will Share, and What They'll Share

As human beings, we **share** for two main reasons. First, we share for **emotional and narcissistic reasons**. We share products and services that make us look cool, smart, virtuous, ahead-of-the-curve, etc. "Look at me! I took my family to Disneyland!," we share on Instagram. "Look at this new technology!," we share on LinkedIn. "I'm outraged about plastics in the ocean," we communicate on Facebook. Sharing makes us look better than our peers, and sharing sends "virtue signals" that we are righteous individuals. A second reason people share is to be a "**helpful expert**" for friends, family, and business colleagues. We share something we find useful (and implicitly or explicitly endorse it), such as an informative article in the *New York Times* on how to cook pancakes or a trick to making Gmail send out auto-responses via "canned emails." We share things that help others, and we share to position ourselves as "helpful experts."

Marketers can "influence the influencers" and "share to the sharers." How? By

1. identifying those likely to share ("influencers" or "superfans");
2. creating easy opportunities to share ("content");
3. and providing incentives to share ("reasons").

For your own marketing plan, you need to translate these three abstractions into specific to-dos.

Take the example of a pizzeria. The owner or marketing manager can identify those most likely to share (e.g., *families having birthday parties, lovers on a first date*, etc.), they can create easy opportunities to share such as table signs and menu notifications which say, "Share your favorite photo to Instagram #Jasonspizza," and they can even provide incentives such as discounts or contests with weekly winners chosen from among those who share to Instagram, Facebook, or Snapchat. Or, take the example of an amusement park like Disneyland or Universal Studios. Identifying those likely to share is pretty easy – anyone with a smartphone, and especially teenagers. Creating opportunities to share is as easy as posting signs around the park of "share spots" at photogenic locations. And providing incentives to share can be as easy as custom hashtags to Instagram (*#disneyland*) as well as discounts or contests.

Another way to encourage sharing is to work with your **superfans** or **influencers** directly. Note this important distinction:

> **Superfans** are customers who love your brand so passionately that they will talk about it and share it online for free or perhaps for "swag."

> **Influencers** are people who have a significant social following as on Instagram, Twitter, or YouTube and who will promote your brand for a fee.

In both cases, you want to identify, nurture, and work with both superfans and influencers to cultivate WOM/eWOM about your brand. The pro of superfans is that they are less expensive; the pro of influencers is that they have greater reach.

How can you cultivate your superfans? Email newsletters, as well as TikTok, Snapchat, or Instagram stories, are ways to allow those who really, really love your brand to follow and engage with you. Recognize your superfans with shout-outs and comments; alert your superfans to special deals or provide "first looks" at new products or services. Give away "swag." Cultivate your superfans by stroking their egos, and offer prompts and incentives for them to share. Brands like

Nike, Harley Davidson, REI, and even Star Wars have nurtured superfans who share and promote their brands for free. Why? Because it gives the fans a sense of cultural community plus narcissistic reasons to share (with each other, with friends, with family, with business colleagues) as well as incentives such as insider looks, discounts, and special offers. Yes, there is some spontaneity to the sharing process, but there is a lot more going on behind the scenes between marketers and customers / fans / superfans to catalyze the sharing process.

Influencers are a special type of sharer, and "influencer marketing" is the term used to describe how marketers identify and work with influencers. First, find your influencers. Any customer can become a fan, any fan can become a superfan, and anyone who has a significant following can be (or already is) an influencer. A **micro-influencer** is a person who has a niche following. It might be the guy or gal who really loves pizza in Palo Alto and blogs, tweets, and shares to Instagram his passion for the "best pizza in the Bay Area." Or it might be a customer who buys your jewelry again and again and is known as the "goto" girl for jewelry by her friends and family. As you identify your superfans, pay attention to which ones are active on social media and which ones have more followers than others. Follow them back, and engage with them on social media. Nurture a community among you (the brand) and your customers, fans, superfans, and influencers.

Next, consider reaching out to the most influential among them and providing them "insider information," special deals, recognition, and even perhaps monetary compensation to be "brand ambassadors."

Larger influencers are those who have larger follower bases and do not necessarily already know about or love your brand. Identify influencers by using tools like Google searches of your keywords plus the word "blog," or by searching social channels like Instagram, Facebook, and Twitter for persons who share content that is close to your brand and who have a significant follower base. A tool like Buzzsumo is invaluable as it can research who shares what on Twitter and how influential they are. Once you've identified potential influencers, reach out to them by email, via Twitter, via LinkedIn, or other mechanisms.

At the end of the day, however, the same conceptual rules apply to influencers as to any type of fan or superfan. Who will share, what will they share, and why will they share? Your job as a marketer in search of influencer marketing opportunities is to answer those three questions. Think "win/win." Like any type of sharer, influencers are incentivized by either narcissistic emotions (*Look at me! I'm cool!*) or utility (*Look at me! I have something useful to share with you*).

Cold hard cash can work, too, as many influencers have taken to seeking monetary compensation for brand endorsements. Especially on blogs, YouTube, Snapchat, and Instagram, today's modern influencers can be "for sale" at the right price. So if you are thinking of paying influencers for brand endorsements, you really want to research whether this or that particular influencer is worth the price and what you'll get for the monetary expenditure of "buying" his or her influence. Some influencers will shamelessly require payment in order to endorse a product or service; others will look for win/win opportunities such as free stuff from you in exchange for a review on their social channels; and still others will be more willing to work with you, at low or no cost, because they truly like your product. Not all influencers are the same level of influence, in the same niche, or have the same attitudes towards "pay to play." It's a bit of a Wild West when it comes to influencers, especially on Instagram. And a lot of influencer marketing today is in violation of FTC rules that require full disclosure if money or free product changes hands. Consult with your legal team if you are giving away free stuff or paying influencers.

For more information on influencer marketing, see **http://jmlinks.com/42r**. Platforms like Izea (**https://izea.com/**) can easily be found by Googling "influencer marketing" or "marketplace of influencers," as there are now brokerage services that connect brands and influencers.

DO: Identify, Nurture, and Incentivize

The **to-dos** here are to **identify** your fans, superfans, and/or influencers, to **nurture** them by creating a positive fan culture around your brand, and finally to **incentivize** them to share by providing opportunities as well as emotional or even financial incentives to share.

The devil, of course, is in the details. Identifying them can mean doing specific Google searches to find bloggers or setting up special email newsletters or Snapchat/Instagram story feeds for superfans or other actions to get your superfans and influencers to "self-identify." Where do they hang out? How can you separate them from your regular customers? The nurturing aspect is creating special communication channels just for them and populating those communications with things that build rapport between you and them, and among them as fans, superfans, and influencers. And the incentive component is deciding what part of your incentive mix will be focused on narcissistic appeals to their egos, which proportion might be discounts or giveaways, and which proportion might be actual paid programs.

Along the way, you have to return to content marketing. The influencer, after all, has to have "something" to share. That can be a product announcement, his or her own review of the product, something newsworthy, a political statement to be "outraged about," a nonprofit to endorse, cause that's worth helping, etc. They have to have a "reason" to talk about and endorse your brand, product, or service. Content marketing with influencers is a two-step dance: step one, excite the influencer on working with you, and step two, work with the influencer to create the content that they can share with their followers.

MEASURE: Are You Generating eWOM and Is it Working?

Measuring old-school WOM was nearly impossible. No one could really say whether neighbor #1 told neighbor #2 to try out your pizza or come to you for their car loan. There were, and still are, incentive programs to encourage customer referrals, but most provide too little incentive to make a difference, and "cash transactions" can look rather sleazy. I don't necessarily want my friends, family, or business colleagues to think I am a "man for hire" when it comes to my recommendations for pizza, cat boarding, or home loans.

In the new "e" environment, however, word-of-mouth can be measured more effectively. If an influencer shares a link to your website on Twitter, for example, you can use Google Analytics to see how much traffic you get from Twitter and from where. You can use tools like Buzzsumo and Pinterest searches to see brand mentions and identify which influencers are actually sharing and influencing and which ones are just taking your free stuff and running away. The "measure" component, therefore, occurs after identification, after a nurturing culture, and after any incentives. Which influencers are influencing? Which sharers are sharing? What content is being shared and why (to look at it from the perspective of the message, not the messenger)? And is any of this building your brand and/or ultimately selling more stuff?

.

Chapter 21
Email Marketing

Email marketing is the "Rodney Dangerfield" of digital marketing. Dangerfield, of course, was an American stand-up comedian with a rather campy, self-deprecating style. He'd say, "Take my wife," and then pause and say, "No, take my wife – *really*, please take my wife." Another famous Dangerfield quip was that he "Don't get no respect." Of course, he was one of the most successful comedians of his day. Like Dangerfield, email marketing doesn't seem to get "any respect." Yet, like Dangerfield, email marketing is far more effective than its trashy brand image implies.

THINK: The Intimacy of Email

Customers may follow you on Twitter, like you on Facebook, or watch you on YouTube. It's not a big deal to "follow" someone on social. It's like meeting up for coffee. But getting customers to give you their email address well, that's another story. And getting them to give their "real" email addresses, not the one used for spam or junk, that's yet one story more. Getting customers to "opt-in" to subscribe to your email alerts is more than just a cheap date. It's intimate. An email sign-up is like a wedding night – they really love you, and they trust you enough to give you access to their email inbox. Those who sign up for your email list are likely to be superfans and micro-influencers, folks who are really "into" you, your brand, or "into" the industry, sector, or topic that you represent.

Think about that for a moment.

The person who is most likely to be willing to give you intimate access to their email inbox is exactly the person who is most likely to be a superfan. And superfans are key to influencer marketing, social shares, and promotion across the entire digital universe. You'd be crazy not to use email marketing. Crazy.

Email marketing is the best way to communicate with your superfans. Better than Facebook, better than Twitter, better than LinkedIn. I'd even argue it's better than your own company trade show because email marketing is available 24/7, and you can communicate with superfans throughout the year. Email, when done well, combines "interrupt" marketing with "permission" marketing. When done well, email means that people want to get your communication and can't wait to be "interrupted" to hear your latest message.

Email is awesome!

But people hate email marketing. It's perceived as spammy and trashy.

Why? That's easy. Because it's so *valuable* and because it's so *vulnerable*, email is heavily abused by spam and spammers. If you think about it, however, you'll realize that the *outrage* against spam and spammers is just the flip side of the *intimacy* of email. People are outraged about spam because spam is, to be blunt, a kind of digital assault. It's a forced interruption into an intimate space, which is why spam is so nasty and terrible, and spammers are just awful, horrible human beings. Spammers and robocallers should be confined to a special circle of Hell.

Flip this around, and you'll see that if you can honestly gain customer permission and earn customer trust, then having a consensual email relationship can be great for both you and your customers. You need their trust and permission. For a great read on this topic, check out Seth Godin's *Permission Marketing* (**http://jmlinks.com/43a**).

Steps to Email Success. How do you use email successfully? First of all, identify what's in it for your audience. Why would a customer sign up for your email list? What's in it for him? Is it a free eBook? A detailed tutorial? Perhaps insider information, special discounts, or free offers? The "reason for subscribing," the reason why they want to receive and read your email list, is the anchor to your email marketing strategy. Start with something free, something compelling, and something non-threatening. Make it clear that you won't spam them. Don't frighten them away with "hard sells." Don't abuse the trust relationship.

Next, there are the technical issues of email – choosing an email provider like AWeber, MailChimp, or Constant Contact, for example. To be honest, there aren't great differences among them. All provide very good technical support. And all provide a lot of good technical help as to how to build lists, create sign-up forms, manage email blasts, unsubscribes, etc. I recommend you use a formal email provider as the technical mechanics of getting your email to recipients, even recipients who have pro-actively subscribed to your list, are not easy.

Third, there's the issue of promotion. How will potential customers and existing customers find out about your list? What will get them excited about signing up? What are the mechanics of signing up? What are the mechanics of unsubscribing so that they feel "safe" subscribing to your list in the first place? Email has content – what's "in" your email eLetter or alerts, and email needs a promotion strategy just like all of social media.

Next, there is the actual sending of the emails. Will it be done on a daily, weekly, or monthly basis? Will it be an email newsletter of one size fits all? Will it be more narrowly customized? Or will it be a **DRIP** campaign? (Drip marketing is the strategy of sending "drips," or pre-written emails automatically via a computer program. Amazon does this all the time – a few days after you make a purchase, you're sent a "please review us" email, for example, and a few days after you browse Amazon, you'll be sent a "you may also like" email. DRIP campaigns can also be set up with eBooks and other free tutorials as the first offer, and then plugs for paid services coming next.) The mechanics have to do with the sign-up, sending, and measurement of email messages and email marketing. You can also segment your list into sublists so that people who like dogs get specific messaging, people who like cats get another set of messages, and people who like iguanas get their own specific content. The more personalized and the more customized you can make your emails, the better.

Finally, realize that email can be used for purposes other than eblasts and "buy my stuff" marketing. It can be used to drive traffic to other social channels. For example, you can use your email list to drive views of a YouTube video. It can be used to promote customer surveys or drive sign-ups to an upcoming Webinar. It can be used as a direct channel to your superfans to spur them to engage with content on other social channels and to share that content to their own followers. It can be used to garner reviews on sites like Google, Airbnb, Avvo, Amazon, or other customer review sites. Email is not an end in itself but rather a means to an end, and email can fit into pretty much any phase of the customer journey.

DO: From the "Reason to Subscribe" to the "You've Got Mail"

Your first **to-do** is to create your "reason to subscribe," meaning to create the content that people will want to get to via your email system. For many companies, these are eBooks, white papers, and other types of beefy content that address customer needs. For others, it is a monthly newsletter that is actually informative with tips, tricks, and industry news. For still others, it's discounts and special deals made available exclusively to email subscribers. What will be your "reasons to subscribe?" What will be the content that is so compelling as to generate the first sign up and then, over time, to keep them interested on a weekly or monthly basis? Email marketing requires content that is truly useful, or users will just unsubscribe and say goodbye.

Second, once you've got a handle on your content, it's time to figure out the mechanics of your email system. Choose a provider such as AWeber, MailChimp, or Constant Contact if you don't already have one. Determine what lists you'll have if it will be more than one, and decide if a DRIP campaign is something that could work for you. Third, figure out how you will promote signups. Plug your email newsletter on your website. Share it on your social media channels. But make sure that the "offer" is clear. Every aspect of promotion must clearly answer the question, "What's in it for me?"

Finally, once you're up and running, send out your emails on a regular basis. If you promise great content, you had better deliver. If you promise a monthly eLetter, you had better deliver it on a monthly basis. *Whatever you promise, you need to deliver.* Email is intimate, and as in all intimate, human relationships, expectations are high. So, perform and deliver. Do not spam, and do let people unsubscribe easily and clearly. (For more information on email marketing, see **http://jmlinks.com/42s**).

MEASURE: Subscribers to Opens to Clicks to Conversions

Email is highly measurable from start to finish.

First and foremost, how many subscribers do you have and to which lists (if you have sublists)? Second, when you send out an email blast, how many "opens" are there, how many click thru's, and how many unsubscribes? This gives you information as to how compelling your content is and whether it's leading customers down the sales funnel towards real sales. All the major email providers such as AWeber, Constant Contact, and Mail Chimp make this easy to see. Finally, email can be easily tracked to website clicks using Google Analytics. Use the Google URL Builder (**http://jmlinks.com/42t**) to track a click from an email list to your website up to and including a conversion in Google Analytics.

Measure the performance of your email marketing, and you'll be amazed at how high the return on investment can be. Just because email "don't get no respect" doesn't mean you can't give it the respect it deserves.

Chapter 22
Personal Selling

Humans evolved to be very sensitive to face-to-face or personal interactions. Even newborns will instinctively turn towards their mother's faces, and people of all ages show a preference for face-to-face interaction. (*Well, except for teenagers who prefer smartphones, but that's a learned behavior*). They say it is easiest to say "no" to an email, next, "no," to a telephone interaction, and hardest to say "no" face to face. Not surprisingly, "personal selling" is one of the most powerful marketing channels. But is personal selling still relevant in the digital age? You bet it is! In fact, you can use *digital* to promote *personal selling* and *face-to-face interactions* to promote *digital*. Personal selling opportunities abound in both the digital and non-digital spaces.

THINK: Expanding Opportunities for Personal Selling

Personal selling has traditionally been defined as marketing opportunities when a salesperson is "face to face" with a potential customer. Personal selling is expensive and time-consuming, so it is usually reserved for high-value, complicated interactions. You buy cars through personal selling. You don't buy chewing gum in this fashion. To the consumer, personal selling, when done well, is seamless. The consumer and salesperson are such "friends" that it's almost as if no selling is happening at all. Think of the best realtor you ever met. Imagine what it feels like to be "sold" a house by that realtor. It's not really like selling; it's more like two friends going out and looking at fabulous houses until they find "the one." That's personal selling at its most efficient, and it can truly be win/win for everyone. The realtor knows the heart and soul of the customer, and the customer is truly grateful to have a salesperson who shows him just what he needs.

But personal selling can be obnoxious when done poorly. A classic example is the car lot, or even worse, the used car lot. When a "prospect" walks on the lot, she's often accosted by a hungry salesperson who begins to grill her on the car she needs, gets her to take a test drive, and then uses "pressure tactics" to get her to sign a purchase or lease agreement right then and there. The "top" salesperson sells her a lemon, gets her to pay an overpriced price and chuckles sinfully as she drives off the lot. Another example is the use of telemarketers. A cold call happens at dinner, and the "friendly" salesperson offers you a Caribbean cruise. It's an offer you "just can't say no to." Except that you do. Even better are personal selling opportunities, as when a friend has a Tupperware party, sells you on Amway, or Mary Kay Cosmetics comes calling. But notice how when it's done well, even a Tupperware party or Mary Kay Cosmetics can feel less like sales and more like friends sharing incredibly useful products that someone really needs.

The best in personal selling blurs the boundaries between friends and business (in a good way); the worst does it in a bad way. Note also that it's situational. If you're invited to a Tupperware party, you expect to be sold. You're going in fully advised. But when you're in the middle of a nice dinner and the phone rings, you really don't expect (or want) to be sold. Intelligent marketing can set up the right situation and right expectations, making personal selling easier.

Another key idea in personal selling is the use of **leads**. Many marketers set up their marketing process, especially but not only their website, so that prospects are encouraged to submit their names, company names, email addresses, and phone numbers in exchange for free downloads, free webinars, software demos, or other "goodies." These sales leads are then handed over to the sales department, which engages in "personal selling" based on following up with these leads. So don't think of marketing as divorced from sales; marketing is everything up to the point of personal selling, and personal selling is at the boundary of marketing and sales. Indeed, one term that was coined around the year 2011 was "smarketing," meaning to combine sales and marketing (see **http://jmlinks.com/43b**). Smarketing argues that you don't want to separate your marketing from your sales or your sales staff from your marketing. Your salespeople are the front lines of your marketing effort – fully supported by an effective marketing plan – yet they are also part of marketing via the use of personal selling techniques.

Break down the personal selling system against the **sales funnel**, and you'll be better able to debug what is going well and what not so well. First, there's *prospecting*. As opposed to waiting passively for customers, personal selling often starts with the salesperson "prospecting," that is doing research to identify "prospects" who might need the company's product or service. This is frequently used in B2B marketing, wherein the company purchases lists and then "cold calls" into a business asking to speak with the "purchasing manager." But prospecting doesn't have to be done in this way; using "free offers" such as webinars, eBooks, or events, the company can entice customers to part with their names, email addresses, and phone numbers, and thus provide "leads" to the sales staff which can follow up by email, phone, or even person-to-person visits. The more a prospect is interested, the less hostility the salesperson will confront at the email, call, or visit. The more the prospect is qualified, the happier they will be with the purchase. So the equation here is for the marketer to do everything in his power to get "qualified leads," meaning leads that are interested in the product and/or service, capable of making a decision, and having the budget necessary to make a purchase not to mention leads that "after the purchase" won't regret what they bought in the first place.

Next comes **face-to-face interaction**. We'll include email, phone, web video, and true face-to-face interaction in this back and forth. Because personal selling is generally used for complex, expensive products or services, the prospect has a lot of questions that need to be answered, and it's the job of the salesperson to know the answers. Indeed, oftentimes products or services are customized to customer needs, so, again, the salesperson has to invest time in learning the personality, needs, and desires of the target customer. The salesperson has to be trained and skilled at anticipating and answering objections and overcoming them in such a way as to motivate the prospect to make a purchase. They have to be good listeners, too, because listening is a technique to make sure that the customer gets what they need and that the sales process is tailored to their concerns.

Third, "**closing**" is the art and science of getting a prospect so excited that they "pull the trigger" and agree to the purchase. Go to your nearest Macy's and watch the cosmetics technicians apply "free" makeup and then listen in as they "sell" the clients on making a purchase or even "upsell" the clients on buying more than necessary. Or dare to walk on the local car lot and go for a "test drive" to experience personal selling in action and the pressure of the close. Some salespeople are naturals, and some are not. All need to be trained in the technical and emotional art of anticipating and overcoming objections to the sale. All need to be trained in the art and science of closing once they have a "hot lead." All need to be educated that the best long-term personal selling strategy is to forge long-term relationships with customers based on real customer needs.

Finally, after the sale comes the **post-sale interaction**. Smart personal selling means smart follow-up, which allows the customer to be "upsold" to additional products or services and builds "relationships" whereby one-time customers become repeat customers or even superfans. For this reason, personal selling is often called "relationship selling" as customers tend to buy from people they have relationships with – not necessarily friends or family but also salespeople such as realtors, car salespeople, insurance rep's, and others from whom they have purchased in the past and liked or respected.

With the advent of the Internet, search engines, and social media, "personal selling" has become intertwined with digital marketing. Don't think of it as "either" personal selling "or" digital marketing, but as "both," and as going in both directions. The personal works with the digital, and the digital works with the personal. Obviously, a website can have an inquiry form to generate qualified leads for personal selling follow up. Obviously, a webinar or eBook can be used as a "lead magnet." But less obviously, a salesperson can ask a happy customer to "please write us a review on Google," or a cashier can ask customers to "follow us on Facebook." A salesperson can invite prospects to a webinar, and a webinar can generate prospects for the salesperson. LinkedIn in the B2B sphere is the digital network for this type of personal selling, both forward and backward. In short, look for opportunities for cross-pollination between digital marketing and personal selling.

DO: Expand Your Definition of Personal Selling

Obviously, identify ways that your digital marketing can generate qualified sales leads for your salespeople. If you have the kind of high-value, complicated product or service that lends itself to personal selling, make sure that your website has an easy "request a quote" link on every page. Make sure that you've brainstormed **"content carrots"** such as free webinars, white papers, eBooks, giveaways, contests, and other collateral that serve as "lead magnets." Most B2B companies use the methodology of high-value web content such as webinars and white papers to get customers to provide names, email addresses, and phone numbers for sales staff to follow up with. Having a webinar or white paper, however, isn't enough. You have to use all your other digital marketing skills such as advertising on Google Ads, social media marketing across networks such as LinkedIn, and paid advertising on Facebook, Twitter, etc., to promote the "free" carrot, drive sign-ups, and fill your sales pipeline. You need compelling content. You need a promotion strategy to get that free offer in front of prospects. You need an easy-to-use sign-up form to capture leads. And you need a sales staff that can do "personal selling" to win the sale. One by itself is necessary but not sufficient.

Focus hard on the need for skilled salespeople, as they put the "person" in "personal selling." You need skilled salespersons who can take the baton in the form of an inquiry from the Web and not drop it. Let's say you had a successful B2B webinar that garnered two hundred attendees, and let's say that the content at the webinar was compelling. Will your sales staff actually follow up with the attendees? However, will they do more than just follow up in a perfunctory manner? Will the email they send out, the phone call they make, or even better the face-to-face meeting they set up further motivate the prospect to sign on the dotted line or not? The to-do here is to train the sales staff in better personal selling, in not being afraid to call and not email, to visit face-to-face and not call, and to sell in such a way that a robust, trustworthy personal relationship is established that makes the sale a "natural." The to-do here can be informal or formal salesmanship training. The to-do here can be telephone scripts and play-acting between "customers" and "sales staff" so that the latter learns how to overcome objections, create trusting relationships, and motivate prospects to become customers. And, after the sale, follow-up needs to occur to "upsell" clients to more profitable products or services and build ongoing relationships that obviate the need for expensive advertising and other marketing efforts.

The *person* in personal selling, in short, isn't at odds with the *digital* in digital marketing. They need to work together. Go up and down the customer journey and identify opportunities where marketing can help sales, sales can help marketing, and personal selling can be carried out by email, phone, web video, and face-to-face interaction.

MEASURE: Don't Waste Your Leads

The easiest thing to measure when it comes to personal selling is lead volume. The next easiest is closed sales. Are your digital assets generating more, or fewer, leads this month than last month? How many sales closed, and what was the value of each sale? What is the "cost per lead" as calculated against the "cost per click" of a Google Ads or Facebook ad? Quantity, however, isn't quality. Not all leads are created equally, so one task in measurement is to work with your sales staff (perhaps using CRM software like SalesForce) to measure not just quantity but quality. Have the sales staff "score" leads against a quality scale measured in terms of the potential value of the sale and the ease against which the personal interaction was begun. A qualified lead from a webinar, for example, might be both higher value and easier to close than a random lead from the website. Not all leads are created equally, and not all leads are as easy to get.

But don't just believe your salespeople. You can hand leads to salespeople on a silver platter, and if they fail to close the sale, the easiest thing for them to do is to blame the failure on a "poor quality lead." Salespeople can be as lazy as any of us and want you (the marketer) to do all the work, finding them the easiest leads to close with the highest values. The lazy salesperson will "cherry-pick" the best leads, close them, and take all the credit while blaming you — the marketing manager or owner — for failing to provide quality leads in sufficient quantity. The "blame game" is not what you want to happen. The toughest measurement task is also the most important: measuring the value that salespeople bring into the process. A *good* salesperson can sell a qualified lead. A *great* salesperson can take a lower quality or less qualified lead and still get a sale out of it. A *really great salesperson* can help you debug the personal selling process from start to finish and get all the pieces to work together. Don't fall into the trap of considering your personal sales relationships an unmeasurable black box.

Finally, because the digital leads into the personal and the personal leads into the digital, measure the cross-pollination of the one to the other. Are your technicians or sales staff asking happy customers to review you on Google, Yelp, and other review sites? Are they getting reviews? Are your cashiers asking for email sign-ups, Facebook likes, and Twitter followers and getting them? Special codes, URLs, and other techniques can measure whether your real-world marketing is generating digital marketing success and, if so, who is responsible for those successes. Reward the technician who gets a positive review on Yelp, bonus the customer service rep who prevents bad reviews, and consider reprimanding the guy or gal who never bothers to care about either. It's a team effort between people and digital, so measure and hold accountable everyone and everything on the team.

Chapter 23
Traditional Marketing

The 1964 musical "Fiddler on the Roof" kicks off with a hit song, "Tradition." Tevye, a poor Jewish milkman with five daughters, starts the number by explaining how everyone should play his or her role as it has "always" been done. "Tradition!" he sings, and then, to his surprise, Tevye spends the rest of the musical lamenting the breakdown of tradition in turn-of-the-century Russia. While there might be a few Tevyes left in today's marketing, I think even the most recalcitrant business owners and marketers now understand that the "traditional" marketing channels are dead, dying, or at least in need of a profound rethinking given the onslaught of digital technologies. With that in mind, let's review traditional marketing media opportunities.

THINK: A New Tradition of Zero-based Budgeting

A **traditional** approach to marketing starts with last year's activities and budgets and uses them as a baseline for this year's activities and budgets. If you spent $10,000 on the print Yellow Pages last year, you spend $10,000 this year; if you spent $20,000 on trade shows last year, you spend $20,000 on trade shows this year and so on and so forth. Like Tevye, you follow tradition and are reluctant to change. A traditional mindset keeps *spending* what was spent in previous years and *doing* what was done in previous years without measuring whether it's working or whether newer alternatives have come along that may be better and cheaper. Traditionalists are among those who scoff at the Internet and can't believe that anyone would turn to Facebook or Yelp when the print Yellow Pages are just so handy and are sure that everyone looks at billboards on the highway.

One enormous challenge when facing a traditionalist is the refusal to measure marketing efforts. How much did it cost to put up that billboard? How can we trace who saw it and who called in about our services? Or, how much did it really cost to go to that trade show – not just in the cost of the booth, but in the cost of employee wages and expenses, and lost time back in the office? How many leads resulted from our efforts? And how does the expense put into advertising in the print Yellow Pages, trade shows, or direct mail compare with the expense of doing online ads on Google or Facebook? Refusing to measure can be as much a problem as that traditionalist mindset that scoffs at doing something as new as SEO for the website, a Facebook ad, or a podcast interview with a journalist just because it's new and strange. Your first step when working with a traditionalist, therefore, might be to create a culture of measurement.

You can't know what works if you aren't measuring.

A "**zero-based budgeting**" approach, in contrast, re-analyzes all efforts and expenditures (both digital and non-digital) as if they were brand new. Every dollar and every drop of blood, sweat, and tears is re-evaluated as if it started at zero. The fact that you went to such-and-such trade conference last year, for example, has no sway as to whether you'll spend the money to go this year. The fact that you invested heavily in billboard advertising or direct mail for the past few years has no bearing as to whether you will do so this year. And even the fact that Facebook organic efforts paid off in 2014 doesn't mean you accept without measurement that they will do so this year and that you'll continue to invest in Facebook as opposed to Instagram or Snapchat.

The key question is ultimately the **return on investment**. A "zero-based budgeting" approach measures the inputs from years past as against the outputs and answers the question, "What was the return on investment?" Marketing isn't always easy to measure, and marketing measurements are far from perfect, but some effort at measurement is made so that you can compare the investment into trade shows, print advertising, Google Ads, Facebook organic and/or ads, Twitter, Snapchat, email marketing and all your marketing channels to assess which ones generated the highest return on investment and which did not. Do more by investing more heavily in your winners and investing less in your losers. For any given channel, ask questions such as the following. Did it help you build your brand? Did it make you money? Did it help you sell more stuff? All of these questions are measured in terms of return on investment, that is, whether one "dollar in" makes you at least "$1.01 out," with some parallel attention to the blood, sweat, tears, and efforts that were also poured in (and cost money in a comparative sense).

With zero-based budgeting in mind, you can compare all your marketing efforts and ask what the possible return on investment has been for one compared to the others. Consider the following non-digital media:

Print media. Magazines, newsletters, and newspapers are dead or nearly dead throughout the country. Both at the mass level (where newspapers and magazines are struggling) and even more at the industry niche level, it's not clear what the survival strategy is for physical print media. Why advertise or put effort into getting into print publications that fewer and fewer people bother to read?

Yellow Pages. Before the Internet, many small businesses would advertise in the print yellow pages. Now, if the print Yellow Pages are delivered to homeowners at all, they usually go straight into the recycle bin or perhaps are used for fireplace kindling. While the Yellow Page reps may argue people still use the print edition, it's the online YP.com website that counts, and the question is whether it is more important than Google or Yelp.

Telemarketing. When everyone had a landline and everyone ate dinner together, that created the opportunity for the 7 o'clock telemarketing call. Robocalls are today's nasty and virulent form of this "traditional" media, and telemarketing still exists in the B2B realm. It's dying but not quite dead yet. The "cold call" may be dead, but used in tandem with digital lead generation through websites, webinars, eBooks, and white papers, telemarketing as a *follow-up mechanism* still seems to have legs.

Direct mail. Direct mail was the first targeted media where marketers could buy address lists based on demographic data. It's still alive yet struggles to capture consumer attention before being dumped in the wastebasket. Do you read your so-called "junk mail?" Yes, no, maybe? What about your customers? Some argue that because so few people use it, direct mail may retain a niche for some types of marketing. If so, try it. But be sure to test it and verify its efficacy.

TV. Americans still consume a lot of television, but Tivo and DVRs killed the commercial, and now on-demand consumption via Netflix, HBO, Amazon, Hulu, and

YouTube mean even less commercial watching. Even worse, the television market is highly fragmented. Live sports are the possible exception, with the Super Bowl being both the #1 sports event of the year and the #1 TV advertising event. But think fast. Do you remember any of the Super Bowl ads from last year? And did any make you like the brand or buy their products? Traditional TV is not dead (yet), but it is clearly being transformed into "on demand" and "digital" TV, often via a paid subscription model with no advertisements meaning no marketing opportunities outside of "product placements."

Radio. *See TV, just more so.* The rise of smartphone music streaming and podcasts has put the writing on the wall for radio. It still reaches people in their cars, but fewer and fewer tune "in," and more and more tune "out." Podcasts, radio apps, and streaming music services seem to be the sharks circling around radio and its imminent demise.

Trade Shows. We've finally come to one traditional medium that seems to be at least alive and even perhaps well. People still crave face-to-face interaction, and people still come to industry events to see the booths, attend the learning sessions, and schmooze with industry contacts, journalists, experts, and colleagues face-to-face. Plus, travel is just plain fun, and with many trade shows located in fun cities like New York, San Francisco, or Chicago, the "excuse" to get out of the office continues to make trade shows worthwhile. Trade shows seem capable of surviving the digital onslaught, so there is at least one old medium that may make it into the new era.

Personal Selling. As explained in Chapter 22, personal selling is very much alive and well in face-to-face interactions in stores and in telephone interaction after some type of qualification or lead-generation process. If a lead is qualified and truly interested in your product or service, it's likely that she will take your call, and she will listen to your message. If she's really interested and you're local, she may even meet with you in person. And if you have a brick-and-mortar store, training your customer-facing personnel to be nice to customers is an obvious to-do. Personal selling integrates well with digital media, and so it makes the "still alive and kicking" list.

Public Relations. Journalists haven't gone away. They still attend trade shows, and they still look for story ideas. So there are real-world opportunities to meet with journalists via trade shows and digital opportunities to meet with them as well via Twitter or LinkedIn. Influencer marketing has "gone digital," but someone somewhere still has to write that blog post or shoot that YouTube video. So if you define PR as the attempt to reach influencers of all types, PR is here to stay.

Word-of-mouth. People haven't stopped asking for and sharing their opinions of products and services with others in the real world. Face-to-face interactions among customers haven't gone away either. But whereas, in days past, word-of-mouth was all analog and offline, today, a lot of word-of-mouth is "e" word-of-mouth. The trick is to figure out how you, as a marketer, can influence word-of-mouth in a positive direction for your brand.

Traditional media is like a dying forest. Many trees are still standing but dead inside (print media, print yellow pages, the cold call), and some are still alive but dying (traditional TV and radio). But there are some old stalwarts that are hanging on if not thriving, such as trade shows, personal selling, and word-of-mouth. And new growth is emerging as digital mixes with analog, as for example, when email or LinkedIn can be used to drive traffic to a real-world trade show. Don't miss the trees for the forest, blindly assuming traditional media to all be dead or dying.

DO: Be Agnostic and Use What Works

The twaggle when working on your media efforts is not between tradition and novelty, but rather to work with both tradition and novelty together. Your first **to-do** is to conduct an audit of all your past (traditional) marketing activities and yet include new (digital) ones. Do you still advertise in the print Yellow Pages? Let me first stop hysterically laughing at you. Then, let me ask you to analyze whether it's working (and how you know that), and if so, keep doing it. If it's not, consider the digital YP.com version or competitors like Yelp or Google Local advertising. The Yellow Pages format lives on at Yelp or Google My Business listings, but that format has gone electronic.

Throughout, audit your efforts and expenditures, both traditional and digital. Think like a customer. Would he or she actually engage with your brand via a print advertisement? By seeing a billboard? By reading a well-constructed business card? Or perhaps at a trade show? Via a Facebook post? Via an email to promote a webinar to capture a lead to allow your sales rep to call to set an appointment to book a sale? Is there data to support that? Traditional media aren't different than digital media – all are about promoting your brand message, and they either work or they don't.

Your next **to-do** is to think out-of-the-box in terms of how traditional media can help digital, and how digital can help traditional media. If you have sales reps either on the phone or face-to-face in brick-and-mortar stores, how can they promote your website or social media accounts to take "one touch" with a customer and convert that to staying top of mind via digital media? Or, if you're at a trade show, how can you encourage people to subscribe to your YouTube channel or connect with your reps on LinkedIn? Get specific. Train your sales rep's to ask prospects and customers to connect with them on LinkedIn. Make it standard operating procedure to film all trade show presentations for YouTube. Be sure that all cashiers know to ask customers to follow you on Facebook or Instagram. Audit your traditional and digital media and look for specific ways you can make them better in their own right or better at cross-pollinating the success of your other marketing channels.

Or, to go from digital to tradition, how can you use LinkedIn to prospect for potential customers, start a conversation, and transition from that conversation to a sale? Train your sales rep's in the use of LinkedIn, that's how. How can you use Twitter to contact journalists, including contacting them before a trade show to meet up in person? There are lots of specific ways digital can help analog. Yet be agnostic between all media efforts, traditional and digital. Audit your available options, make your best guess or learn from what you did in the past, and be open to what's working regardless of format.

MEASURE: Zero-based Budgeting and Measuring What Works

It is, of course, easier to measure digital than analog. It's relatively easy to see which Google ads generated clicks, whether those clicks turned into customers, and how much those customers bought via your e-commerce store. But you can still measure the return-on-investment for traditional media. For ads in print magazines, radio, and TV, you can use "special" or "vanity" phone numbers or URLs to track click-throughs or alert customers to mention special codes for discounts at checkout. You can then track how many codes were used as an estimate for the return on investment from your "traditional" advertising. At trade shows, you can count booth visitors and meetings with key customers or press representatives. Just remember that quality matters as well; a face-to-face meeting with a journalist at a trade show is surely worth more than a phone call or email exchange. And not all data is preserved; some sales will be "unattributable" no matter how refined your tracking. By measuring your return on investment for all media, both traditional and digital, you can use zero-based budgeting to allocate your efforts going forward in a rational manner. What works is what matters, not what you've "traditionally" done.

EPILOGUE

As we come to the end of our marketing journey, it's time to twaggle. To take what we've learned (the theory) and turn it into action (the practice). Download the Marketing Plan worksheets by registering your book. Along the way, some advice: "Never stop learning."

Here are your steps:

1. Read this book.

2. Register your book and access the PDF "Marketing Plan Worksheets."

3. Fill out each section to build out a customized marketing plan.

Then, as you work on a given topic (for example, SEO or email marketing), reference the companion *Marketing Almanac* for pointers to free resources on the Internet. Lifelong learning is key in today's digital marketing environment.

Got questions? I don't charge for short questions, so feel free via **https://jmlinks.com/contact** or visit the JM Internet Group at **https://www.jm-seo.org/**.

Finally, if the spirit moves you, please write a short, honest review of the book on Amazon. Thanks in advance!

~ Jason McDonald

SURVEY OFFER

CLAIM YOUR $5 SURVEY REBATE! HERE'S HOW -

- Visit **http://jmlinks.com/survey**.
- Take a short, simple survey about the book.
- Claim your rebate.

WE WILL THEN -

- Rebate you the $5 via Amazon eGift.

~ $5 REBATE OFFER ~

~ LIMITED TO ONE PER CUSTOMER ~

SUBJECT TO CHANGE WITHOUT NOTICE

RESTRICTIONS APPLY

GOT QUESTIONS? CALL 800-298-4065

Made in the USA
Las Vegas, NV
16 July 2021